PLACE IN RETURN BOX to remove this checkout from your record.
TO AVOID FINES return on or before date due.

DATE DUE	DATE DUE	DATE DUE

MSU Is An Affirmative Action/Equal Opportunity Institution
c:\circ\datedue.pm3-p.1

The Opposition Years

American University Studies

Series IX
History
Vol. 116

PETER LANG
New York • San Francisco • Bern
Frankfurt am Main • Berlin • Wien • Paris

Frank A. Mayer

The Opposition Years

Winston S. Churchill and the Conservative Party, 1945-1951

PETER LANG
New York • San Francisco • Bern
Frankfurt am Main • Berlin • Wien • Paris

Library of Congress Cataloging-in-Publication Data

Mayer, Frank A.
    The opposition years : Winston S. Churchill and
the Conservative Party, 1945-1951 / Frank A. Mayer.
       p. cm. — (American university studies. Series IX,
History ; vol. 116)
    Includes bibliographical references.
    1. Great Britain—Politics and government—
1945-1964. 2. Conservatism—Great Britain—History—
20th century. 3. Churchill, Winston, Sir, 1874-1965.
4. Conservative Party (Great Britain). I. Title.
II. Series.
DA589.7.M39   1992   941.084—dc20   91-4348
ISBN 0-8204-1661-4   CIP
ISSN 0740-0462

Die Deutsche Bibliothek-CIP-Einheitsaufnahme

Mayer, Frank A.:
The opposition years : Winston S. Churchill and the
Conservative Party, 1945-1951 / Frank A. Mayer.—
New York; Berlin; Bern; Frankfurt/M.; Paris; Wien:
Lang, 1992
    (American university studies : Ser. 9, History ; Vol.
116)
    ISBN 0-8204-1661-4
NE: American university studies / 09

The paper in this book meets the guidelines for permanence and
durability of the Committee on Production Guidelines for
Book Longevity of the Council on Library Resources.

© Peter Lang Publishing, Inc., New York 1992

Printed in the United States of America.

This is dedicated to my wife,

Maria E. Mayer,

for her love and care that

inspired me to believe in

my efforts in producing this

study on Winston Churchill.

ACKNOWLEDGMENTS

Although This book is the product of my efforts, it would not have been possible without the cooperation and understanding of many individuals. I want to thank, first of all, Dr. John R. Hubbard of the University of Southern California for his insights and comments; Dr. Lammers, Political Science Department of the University of Southern California; and Dr. Roger Dingman of the History Department of the University of Southern California.

I also want to thank Sir John Colville, Winston Churchill's private secretary, 1940-1955, and Lord Fraser of Kilmurrack, former Deputy Chairman of the Conservative Party, for their comments on Churchill as Conservative Party Leader; historians Lord Robert Blake of Queens College, Oxford and Robert Rhodes James, M. P., for their remarks that guided me to relevant sources; Dr. Sarah Street, Conservative Party Archivist, Bodleian Library, Oxford University; Miss Marian M. Stewart, Archivist, Churchill College, Cambridge University, and Dr. Hobbs of Trinity College Library, Cambridge University for their unending patience and invaluable assistance.

A special word of appreciation to Professor D. McCormack Smyth of York University, Toronto, Canada, and F. Bartlett Watt of the Churchill Society for the Advancement of Parliamentary Democracy for their comments and encouragement, especially their insights on the importance of the Macmillan-Churchill relationship. I have also relied upon the political and economic histories of Paul Addison, Alan Bullock and Alec Cairncross

This writer would also like to thank Chelsea House Publishers for their permission to quote from Robert Rhodes James' *Winston S. Churchill, His Complete Speeches, 1897-1963* (1974).

PREFACE

This work examines Winston S. Churchill's role as leader of the Conservative Party. Only once in a political career, that began during the reign of Queen Victoria and ended in the reign of the present monarch, did Churchill lead any political party. He stood not only as a Conservative, but was also a member of the Liberal and Constitutionalist parties. This change of allegiance formed part of a unique political style that would ultimately allow Churchill to rebuild a Tory Party that had been overwhelmingly rejected by the British electorate in the 1945 General Election.

Winston Churchill was an effective Opposition leader as he was a unique force that saw the Conservatives experience a refashioning of their organizational structure and of their philosophical approaches to the welfare state. The change at the structural level is analyzed in terms of Churchill's relationship with Lord Woolton, the post-war Conservative Party chairman. Selected by Churchill and then encouraged to implement basic reforms, Woolton gave credibility to a Tory Party that by 1951 claimed to represent a progressive and humane commitment to social and economic change.

The appointment by Churchill of Rab Butler to head the Conservative Research Department lead directly to a fundamental shift in Conservative political and economic thought. The dated industrial and social policies of the pre-World War II era were abandoned as novel programs were debated, formulated and then championed as contemporary solutions to the problems of economic growth and industrial organization. It was Churchill's ability to associate the Conservative commitment to this structural and philosophical redirection with his criticism of the policies of the Labour Government that enabled the Tory Party to return to government office by October of 1951.

Table of Contents

INTRODUCTION

In a July 1986 interview in the House of Commons, historian and Tory M. P. Robert Rhodes James told me that Winston Churchill was not an effective Opposition leader. James seemingly preferred a more patrician style of leadership that was personified by Anthony Eden. Yet, he also stated that Churchill should be given credit for two major Conservative Party appointments during his tenure as Opposition spokesman, that of Lord Woolton as party chairman and R. A. B. Butler as head of the Conservative Research Department. James' remarks were part of a series of interviews I conducted in England in order to examine Churchill as Opposition leader. I was also able to speak with former Churchill confidente, Sir John Colville; Conservative Party historian, Lord Robert Blake; and former Deputy Chairman of the Conservative Party, Lord Fraser of Kilmorack. A standard questionnaire (see Appendix) was employed which covered such topics as: (1) The existence or lack of change in postwar Conservative ideals, and (2) Churchill's commitment or opposition to a policy of reorientation. The responses that were elicited provided a broad outline of Churchill's leadership during the five and one-half years of Conservative opposition politics. All four individuals spoke of a basic shift in Tory thinking. Three out of four, James excepted, expressed the opinion that Churchill played an important role in this process of change, which was generated by allowing certain younger members of his party to devote their efforts to the "details" of domestic policy formulation.

Likewise, it was said in the specific areas of policy and party structure that the Conservatives underwent their most noticeable metamorphosis under Churchill's tutelage. In terms of leadership style, Sir John Colville found Churchill to be a dominating Opposition leader, whereas Lord Robert Blake and Lord Fraser perceived him as a leader who "painted with a broad brush"—one content to champion the major tenets of a new progressive Toryism. What emerged from these interviews and research was not only a basic theme of redirection of thought and structure, but a clearer picture of an Opposition leader whose effectiveness can be explained in terms of his selection of political cadres, utilization of their varied talents and his articulation of a remolded Conservative philosophy. Furthermore, in terms of style, Churchill did "paint with a broad brush", as he encouraged his colleagues to argue, formulate and digest the policies of redirection that were developed in the 1945-1951 era.

CHAPTER I

CHURCHILL AND THE POLITICAL PARTY

Was it worth it? The struggle, the labour, the constant rush of affairs, the sacrifice of so many things that make life easy or pleasant—for what? a people's good...

Winston S. Churchill,
Savrola

Much of the historical literature on the career of Winston S. Churchill stops in May of 1945 with the German surrender at Rheims. This kind of analysis emphasizes Churchill the champion of Empire, Churchill the diplomat, or Churchill the victorious war leader. But such historical writing overlooks a unique episode in his political life, that of opposition leader of the Conservative Party from July 1945 to October 1951. Only once in a political career that began during the reign of Queen Victoria and ended in the reign of the current monarch, Elizabeth, did Churchill lead a political party. What is most striking is that he led the Conservatives, whose foreign policy of appeasement had received Churchill's consistent criticism from 1933 to 1939. His vindication discredited the Tory leader Neville Chamberlain and his cabinet. Given the traditional focus of Churchill scholarship, the *Opposition Years, 1945-1951* will attempt to contribute, however imperfectly, to a process of exploring an era during which Churchill, the Tory "outsider" or "rebel", led a defeated party through a period of intense reexamination to electoral victory.

Robert Rhodes James has said that Churchill's character "was his career."[1] One of the challenges of analyzing Churchill's varied career is selecting a major theme or themes that can be employed to define direction. A recent work by Ted Morgan, *Churchill, Young Man in a Hurry, 1874-1915*, finds aggressive ambition as the essential factor behind Churchill's words and actions. However, biographer James C. Humes[2] has criticized this analysis for its limited understanding of the dynamics of British political life.[3] Still, if one looks to Churchill's character, two factors emerge that influenced his politics—a unique form of education and the ideal of "Tory Democracy"—both of which shaped his style of politics and his allegiance to political parties.

Unlike the Conservative Party leaders Arthur Balfour or Neville Chamberlain, who preceded Churchill, he did not receive a university education. It was in India as a young subaltern in the Fourth Hussars, that Churchill realized his Sandhurst training would have to be augmented by a laborious process of self-education. "All through the long glistening middle hours of the Indian day,"[4] wrote Churchill from Bangalore, he read works of history, philosophy, and economics. Gibbon, Macaulay, Plato's *Republic*, the *Politics* of Aristotle, Malthus on *Population*, and Darwin's *Origin of Species*, reacted on an open and curious mind. He recalled that there was "no one to tell me: 'This is discredited or you should read the answers to that by so and so.'"[5] This kind of education, stressing as it did his own insights, developed a critical attitude toward established theories or orthodox thought. He "wanted to think for himself"[6] as Churchill regarded "infallibility of any kind as...totally unacceptable."[7] It was a mind pragmatic in its approach to data, for in considering a problem it was "immaterial to him whether or not it fitted the tenets of a particular doctrine or philosophy."[8] Lord Normanbrook, Secretary to the Cabinet from 1947 to 1962, recalled that during both the Second World War and the postwar years Churchill "kept an open mind...and was ready to listen to arguments on either side."[9]

He would be his own master, never totally at ease with conventional wisdom:

> So far as my own personal cause has been concerned I have mostly acted in politics as I felt I wanted to act. When I have desired to do or say anything and have refrained therefrom through prudence, slothfulness or being dissuaded by others, I have always felt ashamed of myself at the time.[10]

Throughout his political career such independence of thought and action led many in British political circles to stereotype Churchill as a "soldier of fortune, who lives off adventure, loves the fight more than the cause."[11] His lack of awareness of emotions he himself did not share did not help the causes he championed. He would experience the setbacks of what appeared to many in England as a discredited politician.

Winston Churchill's father, Lord Randolph Churchill, had also been judged a discredited politican. The son idealized the father despite the fact that Lord Randolph never showed love or concern towards him.[12] Winston Churchill was not yet twenty-one when his father died in January of 1895. The effect was dramatic: "All my dreams of comradeship with him, of entering Parliament at his side and in his support, were ended. There remained for me only to pursue his aims and vindicate his memory."[13] For three years, 1902 to 1905, the biography of Lord Randolph became his "principal preoccupation."[14] It was by studying the career of his father that Churchill was to espouse the ideal or cause of "Tory Democracy," a concept whose subjective interpretation would color his views on the direction of political reform.

Although the passage of the Reform Act of 1867 had come under the leadership of Benjamin Disraeli, many Conservatives of the 1880's and 1890's—members of the rural constituencies in the House of Commons and those who followed Lord Salisbury in the House of Lords— continued to question the further extension of the franchise to the growing urban working class. However, Lord Randolph dissented from this approach and publicly appealed to the urban workers, thus challenging the landed, aristrocratic leadership of the Tory party. The term used by Churchill in the biography of his father to describe this political clash of wills was "Tory Democracy," a phrase originally invented by Disraeli to address the issue of social reform. Winston Churchill believed that his phrase best described the purpose of his father's actions. In what is known as "Churchillian prose," he observed that at a time "when good Conservatives despaired of the fortunes of their party...to court a working-class vote,"[15] when such thinking was relegating "the Conservative party to the limbo of obsolete ideas, one man who would champion a most unpopular and impolitic national cause...touched the imagination of the English people."[16] The son wrote that his father's "cause" was Tory Democracy, a movement based on Lord Randolph's belief that:

> The Conservative party will never exercise power until it has gained the confidence of the working classes . . .the working classes are quite determined to govern themselves, and will not be either driven or hoodwinked by any class or class interests.[17]

Tory Democracy was the starting point for Winston Churchill's views on domestic reform. It did not include support for socialism or socialists. This kind of Tory Democracy or radicalism belonged to that body of opinion which was not reconciled either to reaction or socialism. In the debate over individualism versus collectivism, Winston Churchill claimed:

> It is not possible to draw a hard-and-fast line between individualism and collectivism. You cannot draw it either in theory or in practice
>
> ...No man can be a collectivist alone or an individualist alone. For some purposes he must be a collectivist, for others he is, and he will for all time remain, an individualist. The whole tendency of civilization is, however, towards the multiplication of the collective function of society.[18]

Winston Churchill sought to be a friend of the working class but an opponent of socialism. At Cheltham on January 22, 1908, he stated:

> Socialist policy would plunge the country into a violent social struggle...Don't let us be content with the existing state of society, with all its anomalies and injustices. Round them off, rub the edges off, and reconstruct on a sound basis.[19]

To Churchill:

> Socialism seeks to pull down wealth...Socialism would destroy private interests...Socialism would kill enterprise...assails the pre-eminence of the individual...consider how barren a philosophy is the creed of absolute collectivism. Equality of reward, irrespective of service rendered...I have never been able to imagine the mechanical heart in the Socialist world which is to replace the ordinary human heart.[20]

His radicalism stressed the fact that "I regard the improvement of the condition of the British people as the main end of modern government."[21] Winston Churchill had "a very lively imaginative sympathy with ordinary people and an intuitive understanding of their attitudes and likely reactions."[22] His concerns to "reconstruct on a sound basis" was translated into legislation while he served as President of the Board of Trade from 1908 to 1910 and then Home Secretary from 1910 to 1912. Winston Churchill led the fight in Parliament to reduce coal miners' hours to a standard eight-hour day. To a miners' demonstration in Perth, Scotland, he said:

> I feel a particular sentiment in regard to the Miners' Eight Hours Bill because—as you perhaps know—my father, the late Lord Randolph Churchill—always supported it, long before it had attained the whole measure of popular strength it now has behind it.... Your cause is a just one, and that out of justice never came harm to anyone.[23]

His efforts to pass minimum wage legislation for "sweated labourers"—the unorganized tailors, shirt-finishers, and sewers—was later to be recognized as "a notable first attempt to introduce the idea of a National minimum into

British labour legislation."[24] These efforts were followed by the establishment of a system of national labour exchanges to address the problem of unemployment. Such exchanges were necessary to alleviate the "plight of the labourer whose whole life and the lives of his wife and children are embarked in a...blind, desperate, and fatalistic gamble with circumstances beyond his comprehension or control."[25] Winston Churchill promoted an unknown twenty-nine year old Oxford don, William Beveridge, to create and coordinate these employment information centers to augment the emerging system of unemployment insurance. William Beveridge felt the drive, determination and commitment of his chief showed "how much the personality of Churchill in a few critical months changed the course of social legislation."[26] The Fabian Beatrice Webb noted in her diary that Churchill's actions at the Board of Trade took the "limelight not merely from [Liberals] but from the Labour Party." Winston Churchill stood out as one of "the most advanced politicians."[27]

In February 1910, Churchill became Home Secretary, the youngest man to serve there except Sir Robert Peel. As head of the criminal justice system, police, prisons, courts, and reform schools came under his jurisdiction. He presented to Parliament a program of penal reform based on the premise that: "The mood and temper of the public in regard to the treatment of crime and criminals is one of the most unfailing tests of the civilization of any country."[28] Under the then existing English law, if one failed to pay a debt—rent to the landlord or a food bill to the merchant—imprisonment was a common remedy, which meant that many working-class men and women were jailed. Winston Churchill eliminated this procedure as, under his bill, such debtors were to be given an extended period of time to liquidate their debts. In 1908-1909 those imprisoned for nonpayment of debt numbered 95,868 in Great Britain. Ten years later, owing to Churchill's reform measures, the number of such offenders numbered 5,624.[29]

When Churchill studied reports showing the age groups of England's prison population, he discovered that many were youths between the ages of 16-26. Further analysis indicated offenses such as stone-throwing and playing football in the streets had led to incarceration. In 1910, 12,376 boys and 1,189 girls were in British jails for this type of "offense." Winston Churchill challenged the conscience of Parliament: "7,000 to 8,000 lads of the poorer classes who are sent to gaol every year for offenses" which if the rich had committed "would not have been subjected to the slightest degree of inconvenience."[30] This process must not be a part of Britain's legal system. His efforts led to the repeal of such laws and together with his streamlining of the procedures for commuting these sentences the number of youths in English jails for these archaic offenses was reduced to 3,474.[31]

Despite his substantial reforms—all made in the face of criticism from factory, shop, or mine owners—Winston Churchill did not enjoy a large following among the working class. The reason for this, in large part, came from his handling of a Welsh miners' strike in November of 1910. In that year between 25,000 and 30,000 miners in the valleys of South Wales struck for higher wages. The protest soon led to widespread riots, with miners wrecking homes and shops. The situation reached confrontational dimensions in a town with that picturesque Welsh name of Tonypandy. There, the local police requested troops be sent to restore the peace. Winston Churchill, as Home Secretary, had jurisdiction over such riots, but he refused to dispatch troops against the workers, for if troops were sent, rifles would be used and families of workers would mourn their dead. Instead, Churchill used a special squad of unarmed police trained in riot control. The looting was stopped and the riot ended but the Home Secretary was condemned by members of the emerging Labour Party for using "too much force." The memory of Tonypandy would haunt his career for the next forty years. It was used by the Labour Party to brand

Churchill as a reactionary, one who was said to be unsympathetic to the ideals of the working class.

Winston Churchill's independent mind and his belief in the cause of Tory Democracy made commitment to any political party difficult. A. G. Gardiner has written that party was only an instrument to Churchill to be used solely for achieving government office.[32] Winston Churchill himself wrote in 1906 what was true of most of his career:

> I found myself differing from both parties in various ways and I was so untutored as to suppose that all I had to do was to think out what was right and express it fearlessly...I thought loyalty in this outweighed all other loyalties.[33]

He did not attach much importance to what he saw as the narrow, confining demands of party discipline, giving instead preeminence to national issues. He had entered Parliament as a Conservative, but unlike many a Tory, he never maintained an admiration for businessmen in government. Winston Churchill "had little confidence in the capacity of people trained in business to be successful in Government."[34] Besides, his father had opposed the Tory Party for much of his career which the son felt had often displayed "an obstinate but apathetic resistance to change."[35] Winston Churchill quit the Tories and became a Liberal in 1903 as he felt little sympathy for the Conservative Party except "in so far as it embodied Lord Randolph's conception of Tory Democracy."[36] Liberals led by Asquith and David Lloyd George were addressing the compelling issue of social reform and as such, offered Churchill a government office (Board of Trade) to implement his own particular views of change and reform. His commitment to cause rather than party reinforced his "outsider" or "rebel" image. Many thought as did his colleague, Lord Birkenhead, that while "Mr. Churchill is unexcelled in the power of lashing the Parliamentary waves to fury, he lacks the not less valuable gift of calming them."[37] He had entered Parliament at the age of twenty-six as a Conservative, then became a Liberal, only to quit the Liberal Party after World War I and seek a seat in the House as a "constitutionalist" in the Abbey Division of Westminster in 1924. The historiography of the 1920's describes an England in search of a politics of normalcy, an ethos not wanting "to be broken by the disturbing force of a Churchill."[38] He lost three elections in succession between 1922 and 1924. The *Times* referred to his candidacy in the 1924 West Leicester election as "an essentially disruptive force."[39] By September of 1924, Churchill had rejoined the Conservative Party, and on April 3, 1925 became Chancellor of the Exchequer in Prime Minister Stanley Baldwin's government. However, Baldwin extended this olive branch only to prevent any possible linkage between Churchill and Baldwin's arch enemy, David Lloyd George.[40]

The post-World War I years saw Churchill's commitment to four major issues which reinforced Tory suspicions toward their newly readmitted member. The first arose out of his position during the General Strike of 1926. As editor of the anti-strike newspaper, the *British Gazette*, his "aim was to beat the strike and he was not squeamish about the means."[41] Winston Churchill abhorred the general disruption of society and condemned the strikers for acting contrary to the national interest. He labeled these workers "the enemy" in the *British Gazette* and demanded an immediate end of the strike. But Prime Minister Baldwin rejected his advice and spoke in less inflammatory terms of fair play and the need for settlement. This did much to ease tensions and end the strike.[42]

The Congress Party of India agitated against its British *raj* in the early thirties. Both Labour and Tory parties were willing to make concessions to the Indian nationalists, a force which Churchill underrated. To him, only British rule could maintain law and order in India, neutralize religious strife between Moslem and Hindu, and protect the lives of thirty-five million Untouchables. Winston Churchill left the Tory Shadow Cabinet when his party rejected as extremist his statement made in Albert Hall on March 18, 1931, that "one would have thought that if there was one cause in the world which the Conservative Party would have hastened to defend, it would be the cause of the British Empire in India."[43] The only supporters he could rally were "elderly, die-hard Tories, to whose policies, in the past, he had been strongly opposed and whose support now discredited him in the eyes of many moderates and liberals."[44] Looked upon by the Labour Party as a menace to social peace and the working man, and by the Conservative Party as a political outcast, many Englishmen were asking, "What sensible man is going to place confidence in Mr. Churchill in any situation which needs cool-headedness, moderation or tact."[45]

Winston Churchill's reputation was further damaged by his support for Edward VIII during the abdication crisis. He asked that the monarch be given "enough time" to find a supposedly proper way out of a most difficult situation. But this stance was rejected by the Tories and manipulated by the powerful press magnate, Lord Beaverbrook, who used this crisis to attack Baldwin, as the Prime Minister had resisted Beaverbrook's widely publicized efforts to create a custom's union of commonwealth nations.[46] Winston Churchill's biographer, Martin Gilbert, described in Volume V a parliamentary scene where Churchill attempted to put his case for the King before the House only to be uniformly shouted down by an enraged Conservative membership that had solidly backed Baldwin's attempts to solve a most delicate constitutional problem.

Winston Churchill's opposition to the appeasement of Hitler is well documented in Gilbert's volume, *Winston S. Churchill, the Prophet of Truth, 1922-1939*, Vol. V. Despite Churchill's correct prognosis, the major thrust of his argument and the events that vindicated his claims were to weaken his party's image as the protector of England's interests. Winston Churchill's attacks on Chamberlain's policy did not lessen Tory perceptions of him as a political Cassandra. Wrote Baldwin:

> I am going to say that when Winston was born lots of fairies swooped down on his cradle with gifts—imagination, eloquence,

industry, ability, and then came a fairy who said, "No one person has a right to so many gifts," picked him up and gave him such a shake and twist that with all these gifts he was denied judgment and wisdom...and that is why, while we delight to listen to him in the House, we do not take his advice.[47]

Even after Hitler had invaded Poland and Churchill was given government office as head of the Admiralty, John Colville wrote in his diary for October 1, 1939: "judging from his [Churchill's] record of untrustworthiness and instability, he may...lead us into the most dangerous paths."[48]

By April 30, 1940, the Conservative M.P. for Chippenham, Henry Channon, noted in his most perceptive diary that there was a growing consensus "that Winston should be Prime Minister as he has more vigour and the country's behind him."[49] After Poland surrendered, Prime Minister Chamberlain attempted a Norwegian campaign but Allied forces had to be withdrawn from Trondheim, Norway, in the face of unexpected German resistance. Prime Minister Chamberlain claimed that Germany had not attained its objectives in Norway, but such remarks now "created disquiet. The House knows very well that it was a major defeat."[50] Winston Churchill, as First Lord of the Admiralty, defended Chamberlain's decision to withdraw but the Labor Party with the House of Commons through Herbert Morrison called for a vote of censure: "I say solemnly that the Prime Minister should give an example of sacrifice because there is nothing which can contribute more to victory in this war than that he should sacrifice the seals of office."[51] Winston Churchill answered back: "Let party interest be ignored, let all our energies be harnessed, let the whole ability and forces of the nation be hurled into the struggle."[52] This speech allowed Chamberlain's government to defeat Morrison's motion as 281 votes were cast for and 200 against, a government majority of 81. Still, a united Conservative Party vote would have given the Prime Minister a majority of 213. As Neville Chamberlain left the House, he was accompanied by cries of "Go! Go! Go!"[53]

Given this vote, the Tory chief whip, David Margesson, now believed that the feeling of his party was "bearing towards Churchill."[54] And yet it was not by a Tory Party's vote of confidence but by the combination of the shock of Hitler's invasion of Holland and Belgium and the Labour Party's Bournemouth Conference decision not to serve under any government led by Chamberlain that made possible Churchill's succession as Prime Minister. Neville Chamberlain had originally hoped to stay at his post until the battle for France ended,[55] but given the march of events he simply announced to a stunned meeting of the War Cabinet that he was tendering his resignation. He did not even tell his shocked colleagues who he favored as his successor.[56] The King's diary records that he thought Foreign Minister Lord Halifax was to be Chamberlain's replacement:

> I, of course, suggested Halifax, but he [Chamberlain] told me that H [Halifax] was not enthusiastic, as being in the Lords he could only act as a shadow or a ghost in the Commons where all the real work took place.... Then I knew that there was only one person whom I could send for to form a Government who had the confidence of the country and that was Winston.[57]

Winston Churchill was sixty-five years old when he became Prime Minister, yet he was not leader of the Conservative Party. He had written to his wife as recently as January 8, 1939, that "these dirty Tory hacks...would like to drive me out of the Party."[58] Yet, his first act as Prime Minister was that of magnanimity to the men of Munich.[59] Lord Halifax remained as Foreign Secretary. Neville Chamberlain was asked to serve as Lord President. No one, Churchill later recalled, "had more right than I to pass a sponge across the past. I therefore resisted disruptive tendencies."[60] However, when he spoke to the House as Prime Minister shorty after assuming office, his warmest welcome had come from the Labour benches. The Tories cheered the loudest when Chamberlain entered the chamber.[61]

It was not until Chamberlain announced his resignation as Party Leader in October 1940, owing to cancer, that the question among Tories was debated "whether or not Churchill should lead the Conservative Party."[62] Winston Churchill consulted with the Whips Office and was told by G. S. Harvie-Watt that "it would be fatal if he did not lead"[63] the largest party in the House of Commons. Yet, Churchill moved cautiously, still suspicious of a party that had rejected his past calls for rearmament and an end to appeasement.[64] When he had originally left the Tories he had corresponded with "Linky," Lord Hugh Cecil, on October 24, 1903, "I hate the Tory Party, their men, their works and their methods. I feel no sort of sympathy with them. I want to be free to defend myself—and I mean to be."[65] Even his wife counselled against taking on the role of party leader.[66] However, he rejected such advice, but in his acceptance speech as Party Leader on October 9, 1940, he did not try to conceal his doubts or his record:

> My life, such as it has been, has been lived for forty years in the public eye, and varying opinions are entertained about it—and about particular phases in it...am I by temperament and conviction able sincerely to identify myself with the main historical conceptions of Toryism, and can I do justice to them spontaneously in speech and action?[67]

Winston Churchill gave the Conservatives an affirmative response. Yet, necessity was the essential ingredient. The Tories needed as their chief one untouched by the shadow of Munich, one capable of leading a nation at war which in large part was brought about by the utter failure of Conservative foreign policy. Winston Churchill needed the backing of Parliament's largest voting bloc. Without such support, Harvie-Watt's prediction would have materialized, but would necessity be enough? Would Churchill, the quintessential political outsider, develop, or perhaps even create, that "temperament and conviction" needed to identify himself "with the main historical conceptions of Toryism"? The fact that the Conservative Party, the party of appeasement, had named its most consistent critic as standard-bearer was symbolic of a process of change that was later to renew its image and philosophy.

Notes

[1] Robert Rhodes James, M.P., "Churchill, the Man," The Fifth Crosby Kemper Lecture, April 27, 1986, Winston Churchill Memorial, Westminster College, Fulton, Missouri.

[2] James C. Humes, *Churchill, Speaker of the Century* (New York: Stein and Day, 1981).

[3] Mr. Humes stated that opinion to this writer in an unrecorded interview on November 2, 1985 at the International Churchill Society Convention held in Boston, Massachussetts.

[4] Winston S. Churchill, *My Early Life, a Roving Commission* (Glasgow: William Collins Sons and Company, Ltd., 1930), p. 117.

[5] Ibid.

[6] Oral History of Sir John Colville, 32 Hyde Park Square, London, July 16, 1986, p. 4.

[7] Sir John Wheeler-Bennett, ed., *Action this Day, Working with Churchill* (London: Macmillan and Company, Ltd., 1968,) p. 74.

[8] Ibid., p. 80

[9] Ibid., p. 28

[10] Winston S. Churchill, *Great Destiny, Sixty Years of the Memorable Events in the Life of the Man of the Century Recounted in His Own Incomparable Words* (New York: G. P. Putnam's Sons, 1962), p. 576.

[11] A. G. Gardiner, *Pillars of Society* (London: J. M. Dent and Sons, Ltd., 1926), p. 156.

[12] Humes, p. 14

[13] Churchill, *My Early Life, a Roving Comission,*, p. 62.

[14]Robert Rhodes James, *Churchill: a Study in Failure 1900-1939* (London: Weidenfeld and Nicolson, 1970). p. 16.

[15]Winston S. Churchill, *Lord Randolph Churchill*, Vol. I (London: Macmillan Company, 1906), p. 274.

[16]Ibid.

[17]Robert Rhodes James, *Lord Randolph Churchill* (London: Weidenfeld and Nicolson, 1959), p. 133.

[18]Winston Churchill, *Liberalism and the Social Problem* (London: Hodder and Stoughton, 1909), pp. 79-80.

[19]Robert Rhodes James, *Winston S. Churchill, His Complete Speeches, 1897-1963*. Vol. I, *1857-1908* (New York: Chelsea House, 1974), p. 875.

[20]Ibid., pp. 1020-1029.

[21]Randolph S. Churchill, *Winston S. Churchill*, Vol. I, *Youth, 1874-1900* (Boston: Houghton Mifflin Company, 1966), p. 431.

[22]Sir John Wheeler-Bennett, ed., *Action this Day, Working with Churchill: Memoirs by Lord Normanbrook, John Colville, Sir John Martin, Sir Ian Jacob, Lord Bridges, Sir Leslie Rowan* (London: Macmillan, 1868), p. 29.

[23]Robert Rhodes James, *Winston S. Churchill, His Complete Speeches, 1897-1963*, Vol. II, *1908-1913* (New York: Chelsea House,, 1974), p. 1070.

[24]Randolph S. Churchill, *Winston S. Churchill*, Vol. II, *Young Statesman, 1901-1914* (Boston: Houghton Mifflin Company, 1967), p. 275.

[25]Ibid., p. 293.

[26]Lord Beveridge, *Power and Influence* (London: Hodder and Stoughton, 1953), p. 87.

[27]Diary of Beatrice Webb as quoted in Randoph S. Churchill's biography, *Winston S. Churchill*, Vol. II,*Young Statesman, 1901-1914*, p. 303.

[28]Sir Leon Radzenowicz, "Some Preliminary Reflections on the Evaluation of Criminal Justice," *Virginia Law Review*, Vol. 63 (1977): 194.

[29]See Randolph S. Churchill, *Winston S. Churchill*, Vol. II, *Young Statesman, 1901-1914,* Chap. 11.

[30]Ibid., p. 376.

[31]Ibid., Chap. 11

[32]A. J. P. Taylor, ed., *Churchill Revised, a Critical Assessment* (New York: The Dial Press,1969), p. 74.

[33]Winston S. Churchill, *My Early Life, a Roving Commission*, p. 375.

[34]Earl of Woolton, *Memoirs* (London: Cassell, 1959), p. 176.

[35]Winston S. Churchill, *Lord Randolph Churchill*, Vol. I, p. 74.

[36]Sir John Wheeler-Bennett, ed., *Action this Day,...Rowan*, p. 73.

[37]Carl Roberts, *Lord Birkenhead, Being an Account of the Life of F. S. Smith, First Earl of Birkenhead* (New York: George H. Doran Company, 1938), p. 198.

[38]Lewis Brook, *Winston Churchill*, Vol. I, *the Years of Preparation, a Biography* (New York: Hawthorn Books, 1958), p. 40.

[39]*Times*, March 6, 1924.

[40]Brood, p. 343.

[41]Ibid., p. 351

[42]See Henry Pelling, *Modern Britain, 1885-1955* (New York: W. W. Norton Company, 1966), pp. 101-102; and Robert Blake, *The Decline of Power, 1915-1964* (London: Paladin, 1986), p. 125.

[43]A. L. Rowse, *The Churchills, from the Death of Marlborough to the Present* (New York: Harper and Brothers, 1958), p. 345.

[44]Martin Gilbert, *Winston S. Churchill*, Vol. V, *the Prophet of Truth, 1922-1939* (Boston: Houghton Mifflin Company, 1977), pp. 466-467.

[45]Victor Wallace Germains, *The Tragedy of Winston Churchill* (London: Hutchinson Company, 1932), p. 280.

[46]A. J. P. Taylor, ed., *Lord Beaverbrook, the Abdication of King Edward VIII* (New York: Atheneum, 1966), p. 41.

[47]Thomas Jones, *A Diary with Letters, 1931-1950* (London: Oxford University Press, 1954), p. 204.

[48]John Colville, *The Fringes of Power, 10 Downing Street Diaries, 1939-1955* (New York: W. W. Norton and Company, 1985), p. 29.

[49]Robert Rhodes James, ed., *Chips, the Diaries of Sir Henry Channon* (London: Weidenfeld and Nicolson, 1967), p. 243.

[50]Nigel Nicolson, ed., *Harold Nicolson, Diaries and Letters, The War Years, 1939-1945* (New York: Atheneum, 1967), p. 75.

[51]Martin Gilbert, *Winston S. Churchill,* Vol. VI, *Finest Hour, 1939-1941* (Boston: Houghton Mifflin Company, 1983), p. 293.

[52]Ibid.

[53]Nicolson, *Harold Nicolson,1939-1945,* p. 79.

[54]David Dilks, ed., *The Diaries of Sir Alexander Cadogan OM, 1938-1945* (London: Putnam, 1971), p. 280.

[55]Viscount Templewood, *Nine Troubled Years* (London: Collins, 1954), p. 432.

[56]Anthony Eden, Earl of Avon, *Memoirs,* Vol. 4, *The Reckoning* (Boston: Houghton Mifflin Company, 1955), p. 98.

[57]John H. Wheeler-Bennett, *King George VI, His Life and Reign* (New York: St. Martin's Press, 1965), pp. 443-444.

[58]Gilbert, *Winston S. Churchill,* Vol. VI, *Finest Hour, 1939-1941,* p. 835.

[59]A. J. P. Taylor, *English History, 1914-1945* (New York: Oxford University Press, 1965), p. 478.

[60]Winston S. Churchill, *The Second World War,* Vol. II, *Their Finest Hour* (Boston: Houghton Mifflin Company, 1944), p. 10.

[61]Ibid., p. 211.

[62]Gilbert, *Winston S. Churchill, Finest Hour,* Vol. VI, *1939-1941,* p. 829.

[63]G. S. Harvie-Watt, *Most of my Life* (London: Collins, 1980), pp. 37-39.

[64]Ibid.

[65]Randolph S. Churchill, *Winston S. Churchill,* Vol. II, *Young Statesman,* p. 70.

[66]Mary Soames, *Clementine Churchill* (Boston: Houghton Mifflin, 1979), pp. 299-300.

[67]Gilbert, *Winston S. Churchill,* Vol. VI, *Finest Hour, 1939-1941,* p. 836.

CHAPTER II

CONSERVATIVE PARTY

"Power has only one duty—to secure the social welfare of the people."

Benjamin Disraeli,
Sybil, or *The Two
Nations*, Book IV,
Chapter XIV.

The first point to be made about the British Conservative Party is that its policy is determined not by select committee or as in the case of the Labour Party by national conference but by its leader.[1] To reconcile an industrial democracy with economic and social inequalities has been the supreme test of contemporary Conservative leadership. The party's commitment to such reconciliation represented a conscious decision to champion the cause of reform against those within its ranks who resisted change. As the party approached the Twentieth Century, it still looked philosophically to Edmund Burke whose "admiration for constitutional tradition, respect for the established religion and belief in evolutionary and organic change"[2] reinforced the party's disbelief in the efficacy of radical institutional remedies for the ills of industrial Britain. Likewise, Conservatives clung to an elitist view that the social order requires hierarchy, that the art of governing can and will be acquired by a few, that good government calls for a governing class trained—perhaps even bred—for the task.[3]

Even though the late Nineteenth Century Tories believed that the ideal social order was privileged and aristocratic, the leadership of Benjamin Disraeli initiated a new legacy: one characterized by domestic reform.

Benjamin Disraeli's domestic policy during the later half of the Nineteenth Century marked a departure from the prevalent laissez-faire orthodoxy of Victorian politics. In many ways Disraeli was a very "un-Victorian" figure, as the Victorian "spirit of strenuous moral effort, belief in progress...confidence in material prosperity struck no echo in his mind."[4] He concluded that successful Conservative policy should be based on the realization that the emerging mass electorate, largely working-class in composition, was bound to insist on social security as an objective of state policy. To "elevate the condition of the people"[5] as opposed to the simple defense of the status quo became his policy. Consequently, a doctrinal devotion to free enterprise did not become as dominant a characteristic of Tory thought as was true of Manchester liberalism. His governments enacted the following social legislation: the Sale of Food and Drug Acts, the first comprehensive regulative laws for the use of hazardous substances;[6] the Public Health Act, which secured the establishment of sanitary authorities throughout Britain; the Artisan Dwellings' Act, which introduced a housing scheme, a novel procedure under which local authorities pulled down slums and reconstructed new buildings mandated for workers;[7] the Merchant Shipping Act that provided for the safety and protection of seamen and gave broad powers to the Board of Trade to detain unsafe vessels; the Conspiracy and Protection of Property Act that extended legal protection for the right to strike, and the Employers' and Workmen's Act which modified the civil law governing breach of contract, making it much less favorable to the employer. Remarked the miner and Lib-Lab M.P., Alexander MacDonald, "the Conservatives have done more for the working classes in five years than the Liberals in fifty."[8] Such measures not only associated Conservatives with the aspirations of the working-class, but allowed the Tories to appear as champions of state authority against the individualism of a British liberalism that had scorned such legislative and administrative intervention. By linking his party to the cause of laborers, artisans and even the poor, Disraeli's leadership created a progressive Tory tradition whereby social security was to be guaranteed by law and backed by state power.

Benjamin Disraeli's efforts to mold his party along social reformist lines was not followed by subsequent Tory leaders. From 1895 to the inter-war era of the 1920's, the record of Conservative advocacy of social reform, whether in power or in opposition, runs very thin.[9] Writing of the two Conservative leaders that came after Disraeli, R. C. K. Ensor found: "They belonged to, they lived in, and they felt themselves charged with, the fortunes of a small privileged class; which for centuries had exercised a sort of collective kingship, and at the bottom of its thinking instinctively believed that it had a divine right to do so."[10]

These leaders—Lord Salisbury and A. J. Balfour— manifested a commitment to the status quo best expressed by Lord Hugh Cecil's *Conservatism*; "Why depart from the known which is safe to the unknown which may be dangerous? Why not let it alone? Why be weary instead of at rest? Why rush into danger instead of staying in safety?"[11] Arthur Balfour, in 1911, gave way to the leadership of Bonar Law, who "personally believed that, for Conservatives, social reform was not on the whole a profitable line to pursue."[12] Under Law, Conservative policy displayed a distrust of state intervention to manage economic forces. These sentiments surfaced in Tory opposition to such liberal reforms as the National Insurance Act of 1911[13] and the Health Insurance Bill of 1912. The latter act represented Britain's initial attempts, however limited, at national health insurance. The Liberal Ministers who piloted the bill through Parliament, David Lloyd George and Winston Churchill, wanted contributions from both employers and employees to finance the plan. To Law's Conservative Party, this smacked of state interference or "compulsion" into the workings of the economic system. Speaking for the Tories, Lord Robert Cecil stated:

> I have a fanatical belief in individual freedom.... I believe it is the corner stone upon which our prosperity and our existence is built, and for my part, I believe that the civic qualities of self-control, self-reliance, and self-respect depend upon individual liberty and the freedom and independence of the people of this country.... For these reasons I am strongly opposed to a compulsory scheme.[14]

Much of the political pattern of the next quarter of a century can be discerned in the electoral results of 1918. It "was essentially a Conservative victory...and the Conservatives were to be the dominant party till 1945."[15]

Young men with the "right" educational background still "went into the Conservative Party, the party with the tradition of ruling, and the party which seemed most likely to go on ruling."[16] At the local constituency level, the party was run by "local people of wealth and influence, and it was an accepted convention that a candidate should pay his own campaign expenses."[17] Such practices produced candidates pledged to support status quo policies. The party's leadership reflected this kind of mentality. From 1920 to 1937, Stanley Baldwin was the standard bearer of the Conservative Party. *The Times* claimed he brought to public life "the fragrance of the fields, the flavour of apple and hazel-nut, all the unpretentious, simple, wholesome, homely but essential qualities."[18] But this kind of leader failed to find the cure for the dominant domestic issue of the inter-war years: mass unemployment. Instead, Baldwin, a man indolent by nature,[19] followed the economic lead of the Bank of England and its Treasury officialdom in the 1920's when determining economic policy, one characterized by restrictive credit and high interest rates.

One result of the 1914-1918 war had been to reduce London's overall international creditor status. The substantial creditor position built up by the Bank of England in the years before 1918 was converted, owing to wartime borrowing and the sale of overseas assets, into a heavy debtor position.[20] Despite this situation, the Bank of England went on behaving as if London was still the unshakable center of the world money market, loaning funds to central European customers.[21] The American stock market crash and financial instability in central Europe created a drain on the Bank's reserves, thus weakening the pound. In pre-war years, Britain weathered such financial crisises by expanding its exports, but in the 1920's England's basic exporting industries were experiencing a long-term decline in demand for British goods. Such products lost their competitive edge when the Conservative Chancellor of the Exchequer, Winston Churchill, decided to restore the pre-war exchange value of the pound in gold. Winston Churchill's first budget, introduced on April 28, 1925, announced the return to the gold standard at the old parity of $4.86 to the pound.[22] At the time, "nearly all persons of authority"[23] endorsed this decision but the effect of revaluing the pound was to increased the cost of British exports to foreign buyers by about ten percent. From 1926 to 1929, the proportion of registered unemployment stood at or just bove ten percent, or from one to one and a half million workers. The collapse of world trade after 1929 intensified the British problem. The regions of basic industry—Wales, Yorkshire, Lancashire, Tyneside, and central Scotland were plagued by jobless men and women.[24] Not only were unemployment levels higher in the 1930's, but there was a sharp increase in the number of people who were unemployed for years rather than months.[25] By the end of 1930, three out of four families in England had incomes of four pounds a week or less.[26]

Coal mining was the symbol of Britain's declining industry. In 1913, it employed over a million men, about one in ten of the working population. Wages were higher than in any other major occupation, expansion was continuous, and coal was the second largest contributor to British exports.[27]

After 1918 and the development of new sources of energy like oil and hydro-electricity, and the loss of foreign markets, such as Russia, the demand for coal fell. By June 30, 1925, British coal owners sought to recover their lost position by closing down unremunerative plants, voiding existing wage agreements, increasing hours and cutting miners' pay. The resulting General Strike not only paralyzed the domestic economy, but worked to undermine whatever progressive image the Conservatives could claim as the Tory-dominated Parliament passed the Trades Disputes Act of May 1927 which declared illegal any strike designed to coerce the government or that was led by individuals who were not themselves employed in the industry concerned. Also, subscriptions by workers given to their union for "political contributions" were now forbidden.

Keith Feiling, Conservative Party historian, has written that Conservative policy is "never intelligible unless it is recognized that the leaders skirmish far ahead of the rank and file."[28] This was true of Stanley Baldwin's economic policy from 1929 to 1937. The election of 1929 gave the Labour Party 288 seats as compared to 260 for the Tories. The younger M. P.'s who spoke in favor of social reforms and activist government economic policies had constituencies in the north of England and it was in these areas, hard hit by unemployment, that the Tories lost ground.[29] Stanley Baldwin knew that by 1929 over 200 Conservative M. P.'s belonged to the Empire Industries Association, an organization formed in 1924 to propagandize for a policy of protection and imperial tariffs.[30] Stanley Baldwin had committed his party to protection in 1923, but this led to electoral defeat.[31] Now, out of power, he advocated the cause of protectionism as the way the Conservatives would reduce unemployment, which was 1,533,000 in January 1930, and 3,731,000 by December of 1930.[32] A new piece of party machinery, the Conservative Research Department, was established by Baldwin's second-in-command, Neville Chamberlain, to study and produce a complete tariff legislative plan. A mass of evidence from industrial managers and union leaders was analyzed[33] that served as the basis for the Abnormal Importation Act of 1931 and the Import Duties Act of 1932.[34]

The collapse of the central European banks led to the July 31, 1931 decision of the German banks to suspend cash payments. This adversely affected the Bank of England, which was heavily committed to financing postwar reconstruction in Germany and central Europe. By October 1931, a quarter of the Bank of England's reserves had been used up. Labour Prime Minister MacDonald and his Cabinet, convinced that the existing gold parity must be preserved felt that cuts in government expenditures, including unemployment benefits would stabilize the pound, reassure foreign creditors of Britain's ability to weather the financial crisis, and shore-up the depressed English economy. A National Government of all parties was formed with Baldwin named as Lord President and Neville Chamberlain as Minister of Health. By September 21, 1931, Britain went off the Gold Standard, causing the value of the pound to fall from $4.86 to $3.40, thus making British goods cheaper. When other gold standard countries retaliated by raising tariffs, Baldwin called for a general election in order to enact the Conservative program of protective tariffs. The October 27, 1931 results were astounding—Conservatives won 471seats in the House of Commons and Labour only 46. Neville Chamberlain was made Chancellor of the Exchequer and engineered protectionist legislation through the Parliament. He also took the first cautious steps toward a policy of monetary expansion. Although he did not lower the interest rate in order to stimulate consumption "among the poorer sections of the community"[35] as was advocated by economist John Maynard Keynes, the rate was lowered from six percent in 1931 to two percent in 1932 and maintained at this rate until 1939.[36] This policy was carried out at the suggestion of the Bank of England but not for the purpose of elevating unemployment. Cheaper money created an inflationary effect and the economy began to grow. Unemployment, three million in January 1933 fell to 1.7 million by January 1937.[37] The unemployment benefit cuts initiated by Prime Minister MacDonald were restored. By 1935, the gross national product recovered its 1929 level and by 1936 imports were back at the 1929 level and even cost 32 percent less.[38]

However much the economy moved away from its depressed base, such improvement proved to be uneven. The areas of declining heavy industry remained blighted by unemployment while in the south and south-east of England, areas of traditional Conservative strength, housing, electrical engineering and the automobile industry experienced growth and high levels of employment. The Tory journal, *The Elector*, spoke of two and one-fourth million more new houses.[39] If Conservative economic policy favored traditional voting areas, the party itself was popularly viewed as belonging to the rich and priviliged. Of the 43 Conservative M. P.'s who died between 1931 and 1938, 38 left estates averaging 218,156 pounds.[40] Eighty percent of the Conservative M. P.'s in that period had gone to private schools, forty percent to Oxford or Cambridge. The corresponding figures for the Labour Party were four and one-half percent and eight percent.[41] In the Parliament of 1935, 181 Tory M. P.'s or 44 percent held 775 directorships in corporations.[42] This privileged class image was reinforced when in 1934 the Conservative controlled Parliament passed the Unemployment Insurance Act of 1934. It has been written of Neville Chamberlain that he was concerned less with what was to be done than how it was to be done. If social legislation is concerned with the transfer of wealth to needy individuals in the population, his care was for the method of payment rather than the alleviation of hardship.[43] By the Act of 1934, Chamberlain intended to centralize all forms of public relief benefits, but to achieve this a new "Means Test" was introduced which meant that an entire household, not just the single unemployed mother or father had to undergo a vigorous investigation by local public assistance committees who verified reported income levels. As one social historian of this era found, "Not only was the inquisitorial nature of the Means Test resented, but also the strain which it placed on family relations."[44]

Stanley Baldwin's political maneuverings and Neville Chamberlain's passion for administrative perfection missed an underlying ethos of social writers, thinkers, and critics of the inter-war years, who "denounced the persistence and aggravation of areas of privation and poverty."[45] Their writings and reports were "given wide prominence in the press."[46] B. S. Rowntree's *Poverty and Progress*, Sir William Crawford's *The People's Food*, R. M. Titmuss's *Poverty and Populations*, and Ellen Wilkinson's *The Town That Was Murdered* presented graphic evidence of large segments of British society that were underfed, ill-housed and unemployed. Such reports lessened the claims of the Conservative-dominated National Government of industrial recovery. W. H. Auden's epitaph of the "dishonest decade,"[47] of an era when political leaders failed to master the problems of production and poverty tarnished the Tory political image. Prior to the beginnings of World War II, the British economy experienced a fifth of its labor force in the coal, cotton, wool, shipbuilding, and iron and steel industries without jobs. Not only were unemployment levels higher in the 1930's, but also there was a sharp increase in the number of people who were unemployed for years rather than months.[48] In the last General Election before the Second World War, that of October 1935, Labour increased its standing in the Parliament to 154 seats (up from 41), while the Conservatives lost 84 seats and reduced their Parliamentary numbers from 471 to 387.

The economic policies pursued by Stanley Baldwin and Neville Chamberlain received little criticism from most Conservatives. However, a small group of younger Tories known as the "YMCA" by their die-hard critics, challenged the dominant, domestic program of the Conservative leaders. Harold Macmillan was the YMCA's most active member. Educated at Eton, and Balliol College, Oxford, Macmillan's comfortable life of the pursuit of learning or of pleasure was dramatically altered by his experience in World War I. As a Grenadier Guard (three times wounded), he came to know the companionship of shared danger and discomfort of the soldiers he led, and felt their contempt for those "gentlemen in England now abed" amidst the suffering and death of the trenches. His social conscience was further awakened by his representation in the 1920's of Stockton-on-Tees, a constituency in the industrial North-East of England. In the years between 1924 and 1929 the level of unemployment in Durham and Northumberland varied between 20 percent and 25 percent, and at the worst point of the depression half the male population of Stockton was without work.[49] Haunted by the specter of broken lives and families, Macmillan dissented from his party's economic policies which he found "intolerable, even on material grounds, that such large resources of men and equipment should rot away unused, when there was so much that needed doing to modernize the 'infrastructure,' if ever we were to prosper again. On humanitarian grounds it was a double crime."[50]

Together with other YMCA members, such as Robert Boothby, John Loder and Oliver Stanley, he co-authored *Industry and the State* in 1927. The subtitle "A Conservative View" challenged his party to modernize its economic thought by accepting programs based on active state intervention in the British economy. Reflecting Macmillan's post-war ethos, the book announced:

> The war period shattered preconceived economic notions, proved possible theoretic impossibilities, removed irremovable barriers, created new and undreamt-of-situations. Yet by far the greater part of the legislation which to-day governs trade and industry dates from before that period. We are surely entitled to ask whether it is now adequate to meet the vastly changed conditions of the modern economic era.

Government alone is in a position to survey the whole field of industry impartially, to judge each industry not only from the economic standpoint but from the point of view of its national utility, to apply remedial measures to the black spots in the national interests, and above all, to safeguard the interests of the consumer as well as those of the producer. The commercial area can therefore not be excluded from the survey of the more important opportunities for Government assistance which these remarks introduce.[51]

Rejecting laissez-faire doctrines as dated and socialistic programs as inefficient and bureucratic, *Industry and the State* advocated expansive credit policies to bring about "better trade and more employment, higher profits and higher wages" which "are an essential side but only one side of the question. We have not merely to put the economic machine in order and let it work its own sweet will; we also want to see better conditions of employment, a higher social standard, and more harmonious relations between various sections of the community."[52] An Economic General Staff to advise and assist the government of the day in manipulating credit and taxation, a National Wage Board, made up of members of capital and labor to stabilize wage rates, depressed areas legislation to create jobs, and a system of co-partnership in industry of management, shareholders and workers "partners" were advanced as programs to create "a social and industrial structure which shall be neither Capitalist nor Socialist, but democratic; where the wage-earner shall be neither slave nor tyrant, but truly, and in the wider sense, partner."[53] Such ideas did not find acceptance among a Baldwin or a Chamberlain. However, they were given more than a hearing by Baldwin's Chancellor of the Exchequer.

Winston Churchill's principal concern on becoming Chancellor of the Exchequer in 1925 was social reform, particularly in the sphere of insurance and pensions.[54] He wanted to see a progressive reduction of income taxes as well as the development of low income housing.[55] On November 28, 1924 he had written to Baldwin's chief aide,

Tom Jones, "I was all for the Liberal measures of social reform in the old days, and I want to push the same sort of measures now."[56] To fund such programs, the British economy would have to produce sufficient revenues. Montague Norman of the Bank of England opposed a cheap money policy and wanted Britain back on the Gold Standard. Few questioned Norman. The Cambridge University economist, J. M. Keynes did:

> A gold standard means, in practice, nothing but to have the same price level and the same money rates (broadly speaking) as the United States.... Our rate of progress is slow at best, and faults in our economic structure, which we could afford to overlook whilst we were racing forward and which the United States can still afford to overlook, are now fatal.[57]

Winston Churchill, never unduly impressed by orthodox opinion of the Bank of England,[58] took note of Keynes' argument. Writing to a Treasury official on February 22, 1925, Churchill felt:

> The Treasury has never, it seems to me, faced the profound significance of what Mr. Keynes calls "the paradox of unemployment amidst dearth." The Governor [Montague Norman] shows himself perfectly happy in the spectacle of Britain possessing the finest credit in the world simultaneously with a million and a quarter unemployed.
>
> The community lacks goods, and a million and a quarter people lack work. It is certainly one of the highest functions of national finance and credit to bridge the gulf between the two.[59]

In the end, Churchill gave way to Montague Norman's opinion of restoring the gold standard which Keynes' pamphlet, *The Economic Consequences of Mr. Churchill,* claimed led to widespread economic dislocation. Given such dismal results, Churchill devoted his efforts as Chancellor to developing programs of economic growth. By May 20, 1927, he had concluded:

> The financial policy of Great Britain since the war has been directed by the Governor of the Bank of England and

distinguished Treasury permanent officials who, amid the repeated changes of Government and of Chancellors, have pursued inflexibly a strict rigid, highly-particularist line of action, entirely satisfactory when judged from within the sphere in which they move and for which they are responsible, and almost entirely unsatisfactory in its reactions upon the wide social, industrial and political spheres.[60]

To develop a distinct program for the 1928 budget, Churchill turned to a YMCA plan which sought to revive industry and reduce unemployment by decreasing the tax rate paid by factories and farmers. In addition, the scheme looked to the Exchequer to help factories modernize their equipment through direct subsidies. This "derating" plan was first presented to Churchill by Macmillan.[61] Harold Macmillan and other young Tory M. P.'s discussed, argued and disagreed with Churchill and with each other as this derating scheme took shape. Harold Macmillan recalled such meetings:

> While other Ministers seemed rather remote and stiff or conventional, anyone thrown into Churchill's presence felt immediately treated as an equal, encouraged to argue and debate like undergraduates amongst themselves, or with a young tutor, with no distinction of rank and without any inhibitions.... All the rest of us would sit round, sometimes late into the night, smoking, drinking and arguing, and of course, listening. The flow of Churchill's rhetoric once it got under way was irresistible. Nevertheless, he quite happily allowed rival themes to be put forward in different parts of the room and took little notice of interruption.[62]

On December 11, 1927, Macmillan sent Churchill a more detailed memo stating, in Keynesian terms, his arguments. Winston Churchill replied on January 5, 1928:

> It is always pleasant to find someone whose mind grasps the essentials and proportion of a large plan. I made you party to it because I was sure you would enrich its preliminary discussion.... If you will call at the Treasury when next you are in London, my private office will show you all my papers on this subject and you can read them there.... I am now planning to

> bring this matter before the Cabinet on the 11th or 12th, and to
> ask for a Committee of five or six to study it with me.[63]

After Macmillan submitted a further memo on the subject,
Churchill replied on January 15, 1928:

> I considered your statement of the pros and cons for the Profit
> Tax versus leaving one-third in the Rates so lucid and well
> balanced that I sent it to the Prime Minister.[64]

Recalled Macmillan, it "was this power to use and
encourage young men as well as to put aside any question of
his dignity when large matters were under discussion that
was for me one of Churchill's greatest attractions."[65] The
derating plan was not to be adopted by the Conservative
leader. The 1929 election slogan of Baldwin was "Safety
First"—this in the face of 1.5 million unemployed. Such
appeals meant to many voters "hanging about the streets or
haunting the factories in despair. Safety meant the dole.
They wanted work."[66] Harold Macmillan lost his seat in
Stockton. Given the lack of imagination displayed by the
party's leadership in the face of such misery, Macmillan "had
to confess, in my heart, that I could not blame them
(voters)."[67] Likewise, the national vote was a blow to the
Conservatives who won only 260 seats (down from 400) as
Labour's would claim 288 seats in the House of Commons,
up from 162. Following the election, Churchill was without
government office and soon to be out of favor with Baldwin
and his successor, Neville Chamberlain. Although
Churchill's energies were now to be devoted to the issue of
appeasement, in the 1930 Romanes Lecture of the University
of Oxford, Churchill echoed the ideals of the YMCA when he
advocated the creation of an "Economic sub-Parliament," to
be made up of professional economists and M. P.'s who
could review national economic issues and formulate
economic policy.

The war years witnessed a public rejection of the
Conservative record of the 1918-1939 era and a
corresponding political comeback of the Labour Party. On

becoming Prime Minister, Churchill faced the predicament of having no party to command in the House of Commons. He had asked Chamberlain to continue as Tory leader and formed his War Cabinet on a national basis. The old ruling circle of Conservatives—Chamberlain (now Lord President), Halifax (Foreign Secretary) were kept, but Macmillan was made a junior minister. Winston Churchill chose Labourites Ernest Bevin as Minister of Labour, Herbert Morrison as Minister of Supply, Hugh Dalton as Minister for Economic Warfare, and the Labour Party Leader, Clement Attlee, as Lord Privy Seal. The Liberal Sir Archibald Sinclair became Secretary of State for Air. By June 1940, Labour occupied eight Ministerial positions out of thirty six, and eight junior Ministerial posts out of thirty five and by March 1942, fourteen junior Ministerial posts out of forty four, and by April 1945, ten Ministerial posts out of thirty two, and seventeen junior Ministerial posts out of forty four.

The key to Labour's future influence was to be seen in the party's representation on the Cabinet sub-committees concerned with social and economic aspects of the war effort. Given their concerns with these issues, the Labour Party distanced itself from its inter-war image that was reflected in its rhetoric of utopian solutions to the problems of peace and disarmament and by its marxist slogans that were advanced as the ultimate cure for unemployment.[68] This change paralleled the growth of a new ethic that developed during the war. In World War I the Conservatives were perceived as patriots working to deliver victory over the Kaiser's Germany. Now they were to be pictured as the party of incompetents and appeasers who hindered the war effort. This image was fostered by the publication on July 6, 1940, of the political satire, *Guilty Men*, a joint effort of journalists Peter Howard of the *Daily Express* and Michael Foot and Frank Owen of the *Evening Standard*. Written while British forces were evacuated from Dunkirk after their defeat on the Western Front, *Guilty Men* accused those who ruled England from 1931 to 1940 of allowing Britain to court disaster by a policy of appeasement. This tract was undoubtedly influential as a *New Chronicle* poll taken on July 13, 1940, showed that 62 percent wanted Chamberlain sacked from government office.[69]

Along with the decline in the appeal of the Conservative Party came the implementation of the planned economy brought about by the demands of the war. As the British population was asked to endure the rigors of war, government now looked to the welfare of all of its citizens. In June 1940, Attlee, who also served as Chairman of the Food Policy Committee, introduced a scheme for free milk to mothers and children under five years. The economy, totally mobilized by Bevin's Labour Ministry and Keynesian methods of fiscal controls, saw unemployment drop to 54,000 in June of 1944. Average wage income rose by over 10 percent in the war years while the average income from property dropped by like amounts.[70] Amid the bombing, conscription and mass migration of workers to defense industries, class barriers weakened as did the sense of "being deprived in relation to higher-income groups which was either absent, or feebly developed. There was no point it seemed thinking along such lines."[71]

Unlike World War I, where the dominant ethic was one of traditional patriotism, with the emphasis upon the duty each man owed his king and country, in World War II the prevailing assumption was that the war was being fought for the benefit of the common people. The hated figure of the conscientious objector of World War I was replaced by those associated with vested interests and privileges. What was emerging was an idealistic theme of "no more distressed areas, no more vast armies of unemployed, no more slums."[72] This mood was best stated by J. B. Priestley in his wartime radio broadcast of July 21, 1940:

> Now, the war, because it demands a huge collective effort is compelling us to change not only our ordinary, social and economic habits, but also our habits of thought. We're actually changing over from the property view to the sense of

community, which simply means that we realize we're all in the
same boat. But, and this is the point, that boat can serve not only
as our defense against Nazi aggression, but as an ark in which
we can all finally land in a better world.[73]

When hostilities commenced with Germany, Labour,
Liberal, and Tories agreed to avoid contesting seats in
Parliamentary-by elections until the end of the war. Between
the spring of 1941 and January of 1943, twenty-eight
Conservative seats fell vacant, but nineteen were contested
by Independent candidates. The Conservatives lost three
seats to Independent candidates who put Chamberlain's
England on the chopping block with slogans of "Democracy
Not Vested Interests" or "Old School Ties!"[74] In the spring of
1942 a poll conducted by *Mass Observation* in three separate
areas of England showed that when voters were asked who
they thought would win the next general election, a majority
favored Labour.[75]

In January of 1941, Churchill appointed Labourite Arthur
Greenwood to head a Cabinet Reconstruction Committee to
prepare programs concerned with postwar employment,
investment, education, and social security.[76] By May 1941,
Greenwood's committee efforts were greatly augmented
when William Beveridge was appointed to head a special
inter-departmental committee to analyze existing national
schemes of social insurance. Supported by Greenwood,
Beveridge began to develop a new outline for a future
welfare state: a national health service, family allowances
and full employment.[77] As these plans gained bureaucratic
momentum, the Labour Party's National Executive set up
thirteen sub-committees of its own which likewise
developed similar programs. Both government and non-
government participants of these committees no longer
viewed the experiences of the inter-war years—
unemployment, lack of health care, poor housing—as
insurmountable obstacles if national and centralized
government planning became public policy. On December 1,
1942, the "Beveridge Report" was published. Claiming that

"Want is only one of five giants in the way of reconstruction and in some ways the easiest to attack, the others are Disease, Ignorance, Squalor and Idleness,"[78] a comprehensive plan of social security for all classes was presented to the nation. Throughout England the press behaved as though the report fell only slightly short of the millennium. A total of 635,000 copies of the report were quickly sold.[79] The reaction of the Labour and Conservative Parties to this "central domestic event of the war"[80] was indicative of future events. Winston Churchill, whose energies during the war years were concentrated as supreme war leader, was busy preparing for the Casablanca Conference in January of 1943.[81] Aware that the Beveridge Report's ideas would have to be carried out in a postwar world where Britain's ability to finance such plans would be limited, he remarked, "The question steals across the mind whether we are not committing our 45 million people to tasks beyond their compass and laying on them burdens beyond their capacity to bear."[82] Given the demands of war, Churchill asked a select committee of Tory M. P.'s under the direction of Ralph Assheton, the Conservative Party Chairman, to report on party-wide reactions to the report. On January 19, 1943, Assheton gave his findings to Churchill. The Conservatives "did not reject it in principle, but their support for it was heavily hedged with qualifications arising out of the expected postwar economic situation."[83] The party accepted children allowances and old age pensions but rejected unemployment insurance benefits pegged to wage rates. Compulsory health insurance that could hinder private medical practice was also turned down by the Conservatives.[84]

In contrast to the Tories, the Labour Party's public response to the Beveridge Report represented a definite endorsement. Clement Attlee pushed the Coalition Government not to defer implementation of the report until after the war. In a memorandum to Churchill, Attlee wrote:

I doubt whether in your inevitable and proper preoccupation with military problems you are fully cognisant of the extent to which decisions must be taken and implemented in the field of postwar reconstruction before the end of the war. It is not that persons of particular political views are seeking to make vast changes. Those changes have already taken place. The changes from peacetime to wartime industry, concentration of industry, the alterations in trade relations with foreign countries...to mention only a few factors, necessitate great readjustments and new departures in the economic and industrial life of the nation.[85]

Ultimately, the Cabinet agreed to accept the Beveridge Report as Sir John Anderson told the House, "I have made it clear that the Government adopt the scheme in principle."[86] Winston Churchill's biographer, Martin Gilbert, in his most recent volume, tells that at the time of Anderson's remarks in February 1943, Churchill expressed the hope that Beveridge's plan would "constitute an essential part of any post-war scheme of national betterment."[87] Although a few Tories led by M. P. Quintin Hogg did advocate the immediate implementation of the Report, it was the Labour Party that introduced motions to make Beveridge's plan a legislative reality.[88] In the month during which Parliament debated whether to reject or pass the Report, six by-elections were held in England and Scotland. The Beveridge Report was the principal issue. Again, Independent candidates who endorsed a national health service or full employment policies cut into the Tory vote which declined by an average of 8.5 percent.[89] Given this reaction, Churchill attempted to reassure the public that the Beveridge Report was not being shelved. Yet his March 21, 1943 broadcast began: "I must warn every one who hears me of a certain, shall I say, unseemliness and also of a danger of its appearing to the world that we here in Britain are diverting our attention to peace, which is still remote, and to the fruits of victory, which have yet to be won."[90] The speech mentioned the need for a Four Year Plan for postwar reconstruction but did not specifically refer to the Beveridge Report. The broadcast aroused a mixed response and did not improve Conservative electoral prospects. When the Gallup poll resumed its analysis of voter preference in July of 1943, Labour's lead over the Tories was estimated to be 11 percent.[91]

From March 1943 to May 1945 the Conservative Party's efforts on the home front seemed to be working at cross purposes. Winston Churchill's efforts were absorbed in the plans for the Normandy invasion and then with the Yalta Conference. Yet, on November 12, 1943, he did appoint the popular Independent Minister of Food, Lord Woolton, to become Minister of Reconstruction with a seat in the War Cabinet.[92] Winston Churchill asked Woolton to produce a postwar legislative package to deal with the problems of "*food, homes* and *work.*"[93] Woolton formed a postwar reconstruction committee, as he was fully aware that when the fighting ended "the public wanted a new heaven and a new earth...the pursuit of war had left a great mass of the people convinced that if the country wanted anything badly enough, it could raise the money to pass it."[94]

From Lord Woolton's committee, made up of such Labourites as Attlee and Bevin and Tories Lord Beaverbrook (Lord Privy Seal) and Brendan Bracken (Minister of Information), emerged blue-prints for a postwar society. In February 1944 came plans for a comprehensive health service, followed in May 1944 by a White Paper on employment which declared:

> The Government accepts as one of their primary aims and responsibilities the maintenance of a high and stable level of employment after the war.... Once the war has been won, we can make a fresh approach...to the task of maintaining a high and stable level of employment.[95]

In June 1944, Lord Woolton lobbied for a Cabinet declaration calling for the building of 100,000 new houses once hostilities stopped. The responsible government department, the Ministry of Health, opposed it, but Woolton found "the Prime Minister was delighted with the idea and gave immediate consent."[96] In August 1944, the

Conservative Rab Butler, despite Churchill's misgivings that such a bill would rekindle party strife,[97] guided through Parliament the Education Bill of 1944 which raised the school leaving age from fourteen to sixteen years and unified the national educational structure.

Such measures were welcomed by a small number of Tory M. P.'s. One was Reginald Maulding, who expressed the hope of progressive Conservatives that:

> The best hope of the Conservatives lies in the rejection of an outmoded conception of freedom, and the adoption of a new positive conception of man's freedom to develop his individual personality in and through his membership in an organized self-governing community, in which the purpose of State control and the guiding principle of its application is the achievement of true freedom.[98]

But such sentiments and actions by a Butler or a Maulding to align their party with the popular cry for reform were few and ineffective. Their attempts were overshadowed by the appearance of such Tory die-hard groups as the Society of Individualists or the National League for Freedom, who publicly criticized the wartime march of events—the expansion of state economic planning, the spread of state services and the growth of social equality.[99] These views were given wider support by Lord Beaverbrook and Bracken. Clement Attlee found their actions on Woolton's Committe so offensive that he wrote to Churchill:

> The conclusions agreed upon by a Committee on which have sat five or six members of the Cabinet and other experienced ministers are then submitted with great deference to the Lord Privy Seal [Beaverbrook] and the Minister of Information [Bracken]...neither of whom has given any serious attention to the subject. When they state their views it is obvious that they do not know anything about it.[100]

The Second World War altered the political landscape of England, which witnessed the emergence of the Labour Party as the recognized advocate of domestic reform. The atmosphere of the home front with its unique blend of egalitarianism and state control mirrored Labour's political philosophy and governmental activities. It was Attlee, not the Conservative leader, who had written in 1944:

> For myself I should, on the practical side, argue for our programme on the basis that the acceptance of the doctrines of abundance, of full employment, and of social security...now be based on a far greater economic equality than obtained in the prewar period and that we have demonstrated in this war that this can be obtained.[101]

The general weakening of class barriers had been accompanied by the belief that government would now be able to achieve what the victorious Coalition Government had achieved—removing the scars of unemployment and the dole. Journalist J. L. Hodson's wartime diary best expressed this hope:

> We've shown in this war that we British don't always muddle through: we've shown we can organize superbly.... No excuse any more for unemployment and slums and underfeeding. Using even half the vision and energy and invention and pulling together we've done in this war, and what is there we cannot do? We've virtually exploded the arguments of old fogies and Better-Notters who said we can't afford this and musn't do that.[102]

The England that was emerging from the war did so with a marked preference to vote against the symbols of the "old fogies and Better-Notters." This was the major political challenge to Churchill and his party. But did the Tories and their leader have the committment to this postwar vision of social reform, or were they still the party of the past?

Notes

[1]Ivor Bulmer-Thomas, "How Conservative Policy is Formed," *The Political Quarterly* 24:2 (April-June, 1953): 190.

[2]Leon D. Epstein, "Politics of British Conservatism," *American Political Science Review*, 48 (1954): 28.

[3]Samuel H. Beer, *Modern British Politics, A Study of Parties and Pressure Groups*, 2nd ed. (London: Faber and Faber, 1969), p. 94.

[4]Robert Blake, *Disraeli* (New York: Anchor Books, 1968), p. 726.

[5]Lord Butler, ed., *The Conservatives, A History from their Origins to 1965* (London: George Allen and Unwin LTD., 1977), p. 100.

[6]Robert Blake, *The Conservative Party from Peel to Thatcher* (London: Fontana Press, 1985), p. 123.

[7]Beer, *Modern British Politics*, p. 263.

[8]W. F. Monypenny and G. E. Buckle, *The Life of Benjamin Disraeli, Earl of Beaconsfield*, 2, rev. ed. (London: 1929), p. 712.

[9]Beer, *Modern British Politics*, p. 271.

[10]R. C. K. Ensor, *England 1870-1914* (Oxford: Clarendon Press, 1935), p. 387.

[11]Lord Hugh Cecil, *Conservatism* (London: Home University Library, 1912).

[12]Robert Blake, *The Unknown Prime Minister: The Life and Times of Andrew Bonar Law, 1858-1923* (London: St. Martin's Press, 1955), p. 140.

[13]Great Britain, Parliament, *Parliamentary Debates* (Lords) 4th Series, 34 (February 14, 1912, Column 35).

[14]Great Britain, Parliament, *Parliamentary Debates* (Lords) 4th Series, 32 (December 6, 1911, Columns 1476-77).

[15]Robert Blake, *The Decline of Power, 1915-1964* (London: Paladine Books, 1986), p. 69.

[16]Arthur Marwick, *Britain in the Century of Total War, War and Peace and Social Change, 1900-1967* (Boston: Little Brown, 1968) p.197

[17]Ibid.

[18]Quoted in Keith Meddlemas and John Barnes, *Baldwin* (London: Weidenfeld and Nicolson, 1969), p. 506.

[19]G. M. Young, *Stanley Baldwin* (London: Rupert Hart Davis, 1952), p. 200.

[20]D. Williams, "London and the 1931 Financial Crisis," *Economic History Review*, 15:2 (April 1963): 519.

[21]Marwick,*Britain in the Century of Total War, War...Change, 1900-1967*, p. 205.

[22]Blake, *The Decline of Power, 1915-1964*, p. 119.

[23]A. T. Youngson, *The British Economy, 1920-1957* (Cambridge: Harvard University Press, 1960), p. 231.

[24]Derek H. Aldcroft, *The Inter-war Economy* (London: Batsford, 1970), p. 85.

[25]Aldcroft, p.85.

[26]George Hutchinson, *Edward Heath, A Personal and Political Biography* (London: Longman, 1973), p. 7.

[27]Blake, *The Decline of Power, 1915-1964*, p. 121.

[28]Keith Feiling, *The Life of Neville Chamberlain* (London: Macmilland and Company Ltd., 1946), p. 161.

[29]Blake, *The Decline of Power, 1915-1964*, p. 281.

[30]Sir Henry Page Croft, *My Life of Strife* (London: Hutchinson, 1948), p. 181.

[31]Young, *Stanley Baldwin*, p. 65.

[32]Blake, *The Decline of Power, 1915-1964*, p. 131.

[33]T. A. Cross, *Lord Swinton* (Oxford: Clarendon Press, 1982), p. 38.

[34]L. S. Amery, *My Political Life, III., The Unforgiving Years, 1929-1940*, (London: Hutchinson, 1953), p. 220.

[35]John Maynard Keynes, *The General Theory of Employment, Interest and Money* (London: Macmillan, 1936), p. 379.

[36]C. L. Mowat, *Britain Between the Wars 1918-1940* (Chicago: University of Chicago Press, 1955), p. 456.

[37]Bentley B. Gilbert, *British Social Policy 1918-1939* (London: Batsford, 1970), p. 196.

[38]Gilbert, p. 196.

[39]*The Elector*, October 1937, p. 4.

[40]Simon Haxey, *Tory M. P.* (London: Victor Gollanez, LTD., 1939), p. 29.

[41]T. F. S. Ross, *Parliamentary Representation* (London: Eyre and Spottiswoode, 1943), pp. 44; 52.

[42]Haxey, *Tory M. P.*, p. 36

[43]Gilbert, *British Social Policy 1918-1939*, p. 196.

[44]Marwick, *Britain in the Century of Total War*, p. 230.

[45]Marwick, p. 223.

[46]Marwick, p. 224.

[47]W. H. Auden, *Poems*, 1930.

[48]Aldroft, *The Inter-War Economy*, p. 147.

[49]Nigel Fisher, *Harold Macmillan* (New York: St. Martin's Press, 1982), p. 24.

[50]Harold Macmillan, *The Past Masters, Politics and Politicians, 1906-1939* (New York: Harper and Row Publishers, 1975), p. 63.

[51]Robert Boothly, John de V. Loder, Harold Macmillan and Oliver Stanley, *Industry and the State, A Conservative View* (London: Macmillan, 1927), pp. 36; 38.

[52]Ibid., p. 134.

[53]Ibid., p. 228.

[54]Martin Gilbert, *Winston S. Churchill*, Vol. V, *The Prophet of Truth, 1922-1939* (Boston: Houghton Mifflin Company, 1977), p. 65.

[55]Gilbert, p. 67.

[56]Gilbert, p. 70.

[57]J. M. Keynes, "The Return Towards Gold," *The Nation* (February 21, 1925).

[58]Macmillan, *The Past Masters, Politics and Politicians, 1906-1939*, p. 112.

[59]Gilbert, *Winston S. Churchill*, Vol. V, p. 98.

[60]Gilbert, p. 238.

[61]Fisher, *Harold Macmillan*, p. 31.

[62]Macmillan, *The Past Master, Politics and Politicians*, 150.

[63]Letter, Winston Churchill to Harold Macmillan, January 5, 1928 as quoted in Macmillan, *The Past Masters, Politics and Politicians*, p. 157.

[64]Letter, Winston Churchill to Harold Macmillan, January 5, 1928 as quoted in Macmillan, *The Past Masters, Politics and Politicians*, p. 157.

[65]Ibid., pp.157-158.

[66]Ibid., p. 64.

[67]Ibid., p. 64.

[68]Robert Skidelsky, *Politicians and the Slump* (London: Macmillan, 1967), p. xii.

[69]Tom Harrison, "Should Leaders Lead?" *New Statesman* (July 13, 1940).

[70]Sidney Pollard, *The Development of the Modern British Economy, 1914-1950* (London: Edward Arnold, 1968), pp. 344-345.

[71]W. G. Runaman, *Relative Deprivation and Social Justice* (London: Roudledge and Paul Kegan, 1966), Ch. 4.

[72]Harold Laski, *Where Do We Go From Here?* (Harmondsworth: Penguin, 1940), p. 88.

[73]J. B. Priestly, *Postcripts* (London: Heineman, 1940), p. 38.

[74]Paul Addison, *The Road to 1945, British Politics and the Second World War* (London: Quartet Books, 1977), p. 131.

[75]Tom Harrison, "Who'll Win?" *Political Quarterly* 15 (1948): 28.

[76]Winston S. Churchill, *The Unrelenting Struggle* (London: Cassell, 1943), pp. 45-46.

[77]Janet Beveridge, *Beveridge and His Plan* (London: Hadden and Stoughton, 1954), pp. 106; 111.

[78]Cmd. 6404, Social Insurance and Allied Services, Para. 8.

[79]Addison, *The Road to 1945, British Politics and the Second World War*, p. 217.

[80]T. F. Lindsay and Michael Harrington, *The Conservative Party* (London: Macmillan, 1974), p. 141.

[81]See Merle Rubin's Review of Martin Gilbert's, *Winston S. Churchill*, Vol. VII, *Road to Victory, 1941-1945, Christian Science Monitor*, January 20, 1987.

[82]Martin Gilbert, *Winston S. Churchill*, Vol. VII, *Road to Victory, 1941-1945* (Boston: Houghton Mifflin Company, 1986), p. 292.

[83]Lindsay and Harrington, *The Conservative Party*, p. 141.

[84]Conservative Research Department Files, Second World War, "Report on the Beveridge Proposals," January 19, 1945 (Oxford: Bodleian Library).

[85]Undated Memo, Attlee to Churchill, Attlee to Churchill (Churchill College, Cambridge), February 2.

[86]Great Britain, Parliament, *Parliamentary Debates* (Commons) 5th Series, 386 (February 16, 1943, Column 1678).

[87]Gilbert, *Winston S. Churchill*, Vol. VII, *Road to Victory, 1941-1945*, p. 292.

[88]Henry Pelling, *Modern Britain, 1885-1945* (New York: W. W. Norton and Company, 1966), p. 153.

[89]Addison, *The Road to 1945, British Politics and the Second World War*, p. 226.

[90]Robert Rhodes James, *Winston S. Churchill, His Complete Speeches 1897-1963*, Vol VII, *1943-1949* (New York: Chelsea House Publishers, 1974), p. 6765.

[91]David Butler and Jennie Freeman, *British Political Facts, 1900-1967* (London: Macmillan, 1968), p. 159.

[92]Earl of Woolton, *Memoirs* (London: Cassell, 1959), p. 259.

[93]Earl of Woolton, *Memoirs*, p. 267.

[94]Ibid., pp. 272-273.

[95]Ibid., p. 283.

[96]Ibid., p. 296.

[97]Lord Butler, *The Art of the Possible, Memoirs* (Boston: Cambert Inc., 1972), p. 115.

[98]*The Spectator*, November 12, 1943 as quoted in Reginald Maulding, *Memoirs* (London: Sidgwick and Jackson, 1978), p. 260.

[99]*Daily Herald*, 17, 1943.

[100]Memorandum, Attlee to Winston Churchill, undated Attlee Papers (Churchill College, Cambridge).

[101]Kenneth Harris, *Attlee* (London: Weidenfeld and Nicolson, 1982), p. 254.

[102]T. L. Hodson, *The Sea and the Land* (London: Gollancz, 1945), p. 238.

CHAPTER III

DEFEAT

I have given him so
much bad advice.

Beaverbrook [On Churchill.]

By the end of 1944, when it was clear that the final defeat of Germany was soon to be realized, the thoughts of the Coalition Government inevitably began to turn towards future political alignments. On October 7, 1944, the Labour Party's National Executive Council, without setting a date for withdrawal from the Coalition Government, stated that Labour would fight the next election as an independent party.[1]

On October 31, 1944, Churchill declared that since Parliament was already in its tenth year, it would be wrong to prolong its life beyond the period of the defeat of Germany.[2] Likewise, differences over the use of British troops in Greece, in addition to specific measures to bring about national health insurance, full employment and other social benefits promised by the Government's Reconstruction White Papers increased political suspicions. On the Conservative side, both Lord Beaverbrook and Brendon Bracken publicly spoused their party's belief in free enterprise by attacking Labour's advocacy of nationalization of British industries. By the spring of 1945, Beaverbrook had pushed aside the mild-mannered party Chairman, Ralph

Assheton, and became the *de facto* party manager.[3] On March 15, 1945, in an address to the Conservative Party Conference at Central Hall, Westminster, Churchill again spoke of the need to arrange for a General Election once hostilities with Germany ended.[4] Encouraged by Beaverbrook, Churchill claimed that any scheme of nationalization of industries would destroy the existing system of British society, since such controls were "designed to favour the accomplishment of totalitarian systems."[5] When on April 7, 1945, the Labourite Minister Ernest Bevin spoke in favor of nationalization and attacked the prewar failure of the Conservative-dominated government in both domestic and foreign affairs, Bracken intensified political feelings by reminding Bevin that his party had opposed conscription and rearmament before the war. As to nationalization:

> Surely the government has enough to do without meddling directly in the management of our trade and industries.... As a nation of entrepreneurs our future is boundless. As a nation of form fillers and restrictionists we have the bleakest of futures. Fears and doubts of our future seem to hag-ride the socialists towards a top-sided totalitarianism.[6]

On April 22, 1945, Rab Butler, Minister of Education, echoed Bracken's thoughts on nationalization when he called for the lessening of governmental controls on industry, to be replaced by an emphasis on "enterprise and risk."[7] Yet Churchill was still able to keep his government of parties together. M. P. Harold Nicolson noted in his diary, "W. S. C. is heckled in the House about recent outbursts by Bevin and Bracken and is asked whether this means the break-up of the Coalition. He replies with good humour and the House rocks."[8]

Germany surrendered on May 8, 1945, and on May 10, Churchill called a meeting of Conservative Ministers, at which all opted for an early election, with the exception of Rab Butler.[9] Beaverbrook and Bracken wanted to exploit Churchill's popularity as victorious war leader to win a snap election. Butler, who had sat on the Conservative Party's

Postwar Problems Committee, knew of its inability to develop a coherent party program. He argued that the Conservatives were not ready for an election in 1945, even venturing the opinion that if an election were held, the results would be disastrous for the Tories. Rab Butler's *Memoirs* leave no doubt that Beaverbrook was critical of this position, even to the point of threatening Butler with political ostracism.[10] Oddly, given what was to follow, Butler claims Churchill agreed with him.[11] Winston Churchill, drawing back from his statement of October 31, 1944, now wanted to continue the Coalition until the defeat of Japan hoping that it would be possible before the Japanese surrender to carry forward the program of reform and social progress Woolton's committee had developed before the German capitulation.[12] On May 18, 1945, he wrote to Attlee: "It would give me great relief if you and your friends were found resolved to carry on with us until a decisive victory has been gained over Japan."[13] But Attlee, under pressure from the Labour Party Conference then meeting in Blackpool to quit the Coalition, wrote to Churchill saying that his party wanted an election in October and would remain in the Coalition only until then.[14] Given this response, on May 23, 1945, Churchill handed his resignation to the King on behalf of himself and the entire government.[15] He also planned to send a letter to Attlee and his former Labour colleagues thanking them for their years of faithful service, but on Beaverbrook's advice no such letter was sent.[16]

Following the resignation of the Coalition Government, Churchill, as leader of the majoity party, formed a "caretaker" Conservative Government pending the outcome of the election which had been set for July 5, 1945. Lord Woolton was asked to serve as Lord President of the Council and Rab Butler became Minister of Labour.[17] Winston Churchill had originally asked Harold Macmillan to become Minister of Labour, but Macmillan declined, claiming his prolonged absence from England during the war disqualified himself for such a vital domestic post.[18] He did accept the office of Secretary of State for Air. Lord Beaverbrook remained as Lord Privy Seal where he directed the Tory campaign.

Traditionally, the Conservatives drew an electoral bonus from the superiority of their organization. The party based its appeal to the voters on an intensively-organized, professional structure that co-ordinated a large network of activists.[20] But the Tory party machine that emerged from the war was in ruins, both centrally and locally, and the party's campaign suffered accordingly. More Conservative M. P.'s and candidates had been on active service than their Labourite opponents. This is reflected in the casualties in the war among Conservative M. P.'s. Of twenty-two M. P.'s killed, twenty-one were Conservatives.[21] The constituency organizations suffered from the absence of so many of their active members in service. Here again, the Labour Party was more fortunate as many of its most influential supporters worked at the home front.[22] The Tory backbenchers or 1922 Committee had warned Churchill of the lack of agents and of constituencies that lacked even candidates to challenge Labour and Liberal candidates.[23] Harold Macmillan recalled that when he returned to his Stockton constituency, "I felt myself almost a stranger at home, and it was so long since I had given any thought to political questions in the narrow sense that I was a little at sea...our local organization had almost completely disappeared in the turmoil of war."[24] Even Beaverbrook, who accepted no interference with his control over the campaign, complained about the absence of a Conservative organization.[25]

The Labour Party, which now challenged the Tories, did not lack in organization or programs. As early as 1943, Mr. Attlee in a debate on the electoral truce at the Annual Conference of the Labour Party declared, "There is no obligation whatever on the members of the Party to abstain from advocating party policy."[26] Unlike the Conservatives, the Labour Party held a party conference every year of the war to which its National Executive report and policy were submitted and debated. Each year of the war the party was encouraged to study its policy, the problems of reconstruction and to prepare their local party constituency organizations for the time when a general election would come.[27] Thus, when the campaign began, the Labour Party, backed by the trade unions, possessed a structure whose membership and influence had been strengthened rather than weakened by the war, while the Conservative organization had almost "melted away."[28]

Labour's strategy in the 1945 election was not one that promised utopias. Clement Attlee wanted the party to "cease to mouth Marxist shibboleths about the proletariat having nothing to lose but their chains."[29] Ex-minister Herbert Morrison, Chairman of both Labour's Policy committee and campaign committee, saw to it that Labour projected itself as the friend not only of the worker, but also of the technician and the professional. He backed his party's efforts to consolidate Labour's representation not only in the industrial areas of Lancashire and Birmingham but also in traditional Tory rural and middle-class constituencies.[30] In April, Labour's campaign statement, *Let us Face the Future*, was published and was made available for study by all future candidates. The party pledged that, if victorious in the postwar election, it would nationalize the Bank of England, fuel and power, inland transport, and the iron and steel industries. Full employment was to be supported through the maintenance of purchasing power by government, a national health service and social security schemes would be implemented, and Butler's Education Act was to be put into practice as soon as Germany surrendered.[31] This program received wide voter approval, and according to opinion polls, a majority approved of its nationalization and social security pledges.[32]

The Conservative strategy was a different matter. There were voices raised that tried to give the Tories a progressive, forward-looking appeal. Lord Woolton on May 31, 1945, wrote to Lord Beaverbrook with the following plan:

People wonder whether the great war leader will be a good peace leader: "is he really interested in reconstruction and social reform" is the question that I find people asking.

To meet this we ought, as a Government, to come out with a statement of what we intend to do about these things. Let us tell the public that we shall build houses through municipalities, that we shall also build them through the free enterprise of the building trades, who, in fact, did most of the home building before the war.

We ought to take—as is our due—the credit for the Health Service and National Insurance proposals.... The White Paper on Employment is the best thing we produced in my late office, and some properly chosen language about the Government taking these steps to prevent unemployment before it arises will have great effect....

I believe that the mixture we want is Churchill the war-winner, Churchill, the British bull-dog breed in international conferences, and Churchill, the leader of a Government with a programme of social reform that will ease the hard-pressed and raise the standard of life for all.[33]

Likewise, on June 6, 1945, Butler and the Conservative Postwar Problems Committee presented to Churchill a report entitled, "Forty Years of Progress." It spoke of the following Tory achievements:

From 1935 to 1939 the building industry was adding new houses at the rate of over 350,000 permanent houses a year; the new Education Bill [of 1944] sponsored by a Conservative Minister, guarantees an even more spectacular and far-reaching improvement; we rightly see in the expansion of the social services as a State responsibility a useful measure of the social progress of this last half-century.[34]

Yet, Churchill, Beaverbrook and the hard-line Conservatives did not accept such views. Harold Macmillan described the new government as one of "a certain flatness and frustration.... We knew that were were indeed 'caretakers' and that our main task was to do our best to keep the house in order until the duly elected tenant—whoever he might be—returned to claim his rights."[35]

Winston Churchill, responding to Beaverbrook's advice and fortified in his apprehension of socialist philosophy by reading Professor F. A. Hayek's anti-socialist book, *The Road to Serfdom*,[36] set the tone of the Tory campaign in his first election broadcast of June 6, 1945:

> My friends, I must tell you that a Socialist policy is abhorent to British ideas of freedom.... There can be no doubt that Socialism is inseparably interwoven with totalitarianism.... Socialism is in its essense an attack not only upon British enterprise, but upon the right of a man or woman to breathe freely without having a harsh, clumsy, tyrannical hand clasped across their mouth and nostrils. A free Parliament—look at that—a free Parliament is odious to the Socialist doctrine.... I declare to you, from the bottom of my heart, that no Socialist system can be established without a political police.... They would have to fall back on some sort of Gestapo, no doubt very humanely directed in the first instance...it would gather all the power to the supreme party and the party leaders, rising like stately pinnacles above their vast bureaucracies of civil servants, no longer servants and no longer civil.[37]

This approach allowed Attlee to project Labour's pragmatic image as in his reply speech he claimed:

> When I listened to the Prime Minister's speech last night in which he gave such a travesty of the policy of the Labour Party, I realised at once what was his object. He wanted the electors to understand how great was the difference between Winston Churchill the great leader in war of a united nation, and Mr. Churchill the party leader of the Conservatives. He feared lest those who had accepted his leadership in war might be tempted out of gratitude to follow him further. I thank him for having disillusioned them so thoroughly. The voice we heard last night was that of Mr. Churchill, but the mind was that of Lord Beaverbrook.[38]

This measured response allowed the Labour Party to deflate the Churchill image of the steady, trustworthy leader. Ex-minister Morrison asked why Churchill had appointed him Home Secretary in 1940, thus in charge of the British police forces, if he seriously believed that as a socialist he was supposedly in favour of a Gestapo.[39]

By attacking "socialism" in the abstract, the Tories did not offer reasoned criticism of *Let us Face the Future*. This strategy was further reinforced when on June 14, 1945, Churchill invited Mr. Attlee to accompany the Prime Minister to the first meeting of the Big Three in Potsdam. The Chairman of the National Executive of the Labour Party, Harold Laski, while agreeing that Attlee should go to Germany as an observer, issued a public statement:

> The Labour Party cannot be committed to any decision arrived at by the Three Power Conference where matters will be discussed which have not been debated either in the Party Executive or at meetings of the Parliamentary Labour Party.[40]

Winston Churchill then published a letter to Mr. Attlee:

> My idea was that you should come as friend and counsellor.... Merely to come as a mute observer would, I think, be derogatory to your position as leader of your party.[41]

Brendon Bracken took up the attack:

> We believed that there was a broad measure of agreement between the Socialist Party and the National Government in carrying forward to a conclusion the policy of the great Churchill Coalition. But Mr. Harold Laski, Chairman of the Socialist Party, says that his party cannot be committed by any decision reached at the Three-Power Conference. We are now advised in plain terms that a continuing foreign policy is something we can no longer take for granted. It becomes the task of the electors in these conditions not merely to send Mr. Churchill...to the Conference with a massive vote of confidence, but also to determine that the known and approved policy of the Coalition shall continue, and that it shall not be supplanted by some untried and unknown...policy of the Socialist party.[42]

Lord Beaverbrook went even further:

> I hereby declare that Laski is aiming at the destruction of the Parliamentary system of Great Britain and that he hopes to set up in its place the dictatorship of something commonly called the "National Executive."[43]

Mr. Attlee's response to these Conservative maneuverings was typical of the Labour Party's image of restraint and caution:

> During the whole of the time...my position as the responsible spokesman of the Labour Party and my devotion to democratic principles have never been challenged. I can afford, therefore, to ignore the eleventh-hour insinuations and misrepresentations to which...the Prime Minister has lent his support.[44]

Despite the time and effort devoted to the "Laski affair," the great mass of the electorate took little notice of it.[45] In their study of the election, R. B. McCallum and Alison Readman found that what mattered most to the voters were domestic issues and how the Tories had handled jobs, housing and social services. The Tories, who had exercised power throughout most of the inter-war years had "all the evils of this unhappy period laid at the door of the Conservative Party."[46] The Conservative election manifesto, *Mr. Churchill's Declaration of Policy*, was a mere twenty page document. Its emphasis was not housing or health care but international affairs. Its introduction stated:

> Britain is still at war, and must not turn aside from the vast further efforts still needed to bring Japan to the same end as Germany. Even when all foreign enemies are utterly defeated, that will not be the end of our task. It will be the beginning of our further opportunity—the opportunity which we snatched out of the jaws of disaster in 1940 to save the world from tyranny and then to play our part in its wise and helpful guidance.[47]

However, Labour had countered this appeal by streesing the issue of housing. Ernest Bevin caught the electorate's ear by pledging that once his party was in power, it would build four to five million new homes.[48] Again, polls demonstrated the importance of such appeals. A *News Chronicle* Gallup Poll of June 11, 1945, showed that 41 percent of those asked said housing was the major item of interest, followed by full employment (15 percent) and social security (7 percent).[49] Winston Churchill's tour of England in June 1945, where he was received by huge crowds throughout the country, lured Conservatives into believing that by emphasizing Churchill's international reputation and their anti-socialist attacks, that such a strategy could be translated into electoral victory. Besides, the *Birmingham Post* carried the headline, "Premier's Triumphal Tour of the Midland's, Nine Hours in Blazing Sunshine"[50] while the *Glasgow Herald* noted, "The carnival appearance of the streets through which the Premier passed was reminiscent of V E Day."[51] This kind of reporting seemed to point to yet another Conservative victory. Thus, Churchill, reading the outward signs of crowd enthusiasm as voter approval of the Tory Party, again stressed in the last days before the election the dangers of entrusting the Government of England to a party and a leader whose decisions might be nullified by a national party executive committee presided over by Mr. Laski.[52] He concluded his campaign by stating that the defeat of Japan was to be his new government's "first practical business."[53] The campaign over, Churchill was told by Beaverbrook that the Tories would win the election with a comfortable majority.[54] Confident of victory, Churchill retired to Hendaye, France, near the Spanish frontier, to await what was said to be a predictable outcome.

Instead of victory for the Tories, the General Election of 1945 was one of the greatest turnovers in Parliamentary history since the Great Reform Bill of 1832. Only twice had the Tories been so reduced in Parliamentary seats, 1832 and 1906. Labour won 393 seats to the Conservatives 189. Of their 209 net gains, 79 seats were in constituencies which never had elected a Labour M. P.[55] The Tory vote fell from 55 percent in the 1935 General Election to 40 percent in 1945.[56] Labour's percentage rose from 41 percent in 1935 to 50 percent,[57] a gain of 12 percent, which meant the loss by the Conservatives of a quarter of their supporters. One of the more insightful commentaries of the election appeared at the end of July in *The Times*:

> When all allowance has been made for the emergence of a new generation of voters and for the "swing of the pendulum" among

the old, it will still be necessary to seek the explanation of the
Conservative defeat largely in the circumstances and conduct of
the election itself. Mr. Churchill himself introduced and insisted
on emphasising the narrower animosities of the party fight. As a
result the great national programme was allowed to step into the
background.[58]

The "Gestapo" speech and Beaverbrook's strategy all
worked to harm the Conservative electoral fortunes. But this
failure of tactics obscured the main weakness of the
Conservative Party—a lack of an effective organization to
mobilize its strength and a contemporary philosophy that
could appeal to an England whose priorities now required
the benefits which only the welfare state could supply. As
Churchill and the Conservatives entered the Opposition
Years, the crucial test of their political survival would be the
ability to recognize this weakness and to make a
commitment to reorganize a party that would be responsive
to the ideals of a postwar society.

Notes

[1] Report of the 43rd Annual Conference of the Labour Party, December
11-15, 1944, p. 37.

[2] Great Britain, Parliament, *Parliamentary Debates* (Commons) 5th Series,
404 (October 31, 1944, Column 662).

[3] A. T. P. Taylor, *Beaverbrook* (London: Hanush Hamilton, 1972), p. 564.

[4] Butler Papers, RAB G17, 1-243, 1945; March 1945 (Trinity College,
Cambridge).

[5] Harris, *Attlee*, p. 248.

[6] *The Times*, April 10, 1945.

[7] Butler Papers, RAB G17, 1-243.

[8] Nicolson, *Harold Nicolson, Diaries and Letters: The War Years, 1939-1945*,
p. 446.

[9] Lord Butler, *The Art of the Possible, Memoirs* (Boston: Gambit
Incorporated, 1972), p. 127.

[10]Butler, p. 127.

[11]Ibid.

[12]Harold Macmillan, *Tides of Fortune, 1945-1955* (London: Macmillan, 1969), p. 26.

[13]Philip Goodhart with Ursula Branston, *The 1922, The Story of the Conservative Backbenchers' Parliamentary Committee* (London: Macmillan, 1973), p. 137.

[14]Harris, *Attlee*, p. 250.

[15]Woolton Papers, Box 20, Correspondence and Papers as Lord President of the Council, May-July, 1945 (Bodleian Library, Oxford).

[16]John Colville, *Winston Churchill and His Inner Circle* (New York: Wyndham Books, 1981), p. 109.

[17]Woolton Papers, Box 20, Correspondence and Papers as Lord President of the Council, May-July, 1945 (Bodleian Library, Oxford).

[18]Macmillan, *Tides of Fortune, 1945-1955*, p. 28.

[19]Kenneth Young, *Churchill and Beaverbrook, A Study in Friendship and Politics* (New York: James H. Heineman, Inc., 1966), p. 266.

[20]Lord Butler, ed., *The Conservatives, A History from Their Origins to 1965* (London: George Allen and Unwin LTD., 1977), p. 419.

[21]Earl Winterton, *Orders of the Day* (London: Cassell and Company LTD., 1953), p. 315.

[22]Ibid.

[23]Goodhart with Branston, *The 1922, The Story of the Conservative Backbenchers' Parliamentary Committee*, p. 137.

[24]Macmillan, *Tides of Fortune, 1945-1955*, pp. 30-31.

[25]Young, *Churchill and Beaverbrook, A Study in Friendship and Politics*, pp. 266-267.

[26]Report of the Annual Conference of the Labour Party, 1943, p. 127.

[27]R. B. McCallum and Alison Reademan, *The British General Election of 1945* (London: Oxford University Press, 1947), p. 5.

[28]Macmillan, *Tides of Fortune, 1945-1955*, p. 25.

[29]Undated Memo, Attlee Papers (Churchill College, Cambridge), January 24.

[30]McCallum and Reademan, *The British General Election of 1945*, p. 129.

[31]*Let Us Face the Future*, April 1945.

[32]Frank V. Cantwell, "The Meaning of the British Election," *Public Opinion Quarterly* 9 (1945): 156.

[33]Woolton Papers, M. S. Woolton, Box 20, Correspondence and Papers of Lord Woolton, Letter, Lord Woolton to Lord Beaverbrook May 31, 1945 (Bodleian Library, Oxford).

[34]Butler Papers, RAB G17, 1-243, 1945 (Trinity College, Cambridge).

[35]Macmillan, *Tides of Fortune, 1945-1955*, p. 29.

[36]Macmillan, p. 31.

[37]*The Listener*, June 7, 1945, p. 629.

[38]*The Listener*, June 14, 1945, p. 616.

[39]*The Times*, June 20, 1945.

[40]*The Times*, June 15, 1945.

[41]*The Times*, June 16, 1945.

[42]*The Listener*, June 21, 1945, p. 688.

[43]*The Daily Express*, June 20, 1945.

[44]*The Times*, June 25, 1945.

[45]McCallum and Reademan, *The British General Election of 1945*, p. 149.

[46]McCallum and Reademan, p. 44.

[47]*Mr. Churchill's Declaration of Policy to the Electors*, p. 1.

[48]*The Times*, June 18, 1945.

[49]*News Chronicle*, June 11, 1945.

[50]*Birmingham Post*, June 26, 1945.

[51]*Glasglow Herald*, June 29, 1945.

[52]McCallum and Reademan, *The British General Election of 1945*, p. 173.

[53]James, *Winston S. Churchill, His Complete Speeches, 1897-1963*, Vol. VII, *1943-1949*, p. 7201.

[54]Young, *Churchill and Beaverbrook, A Study in Friendship and Politics*, p. 268.

[55]McCallum and Reademan, p. 261.

[56]McCallum and Reademan, p. 264.

[57]Ibid.

[58]Article of *The Times* as quoted in Lord Butler, ed., *The Conservatives, A History from Their Origins to 1965* (London: George Allen and Unwin LTD., 1977), p. 413.

CHAPTER IV

NEW DIRECTIONS

"'ABEUNT STUDIA IN MORES,'
practices zealously pursued pass into habits."

On the day after the General Election of 1945, the cabinet met and Harold Macmillan recalled that Churchill appeared somewhat "dazed by the blow."[1] Five Cabinet Ministers and twenty-six junior Ministers had lost their Parliamentary seats.[2] Gone were Bracken and Macmillan. As one survivor recalled, "Few of us on the sparsely occupied Conservative benches dared to hope or had any reason to hope—that this vast overwhelming majority would be wiped off within five years, or that within another six years, we should enter office and hold it, with ever increasing majorities, for the following decade."[3]

The Earl of Selborne expressed a widely held opinion of many defeated Tories when he wrote to Churchill on July 30, 1945, that the "ingratitude of the electorate has staggered me and makes me boil with indignation."[4] Yet, those who had been elected were not of the old, prewar cast. Of the 189 Tories who sat in the new Parliament, 78 had not been members of the previous House.[5] Even in terms of age, the Conservatives were of a younger age, averaging 41 years and four months to Labour M. P.'s 45 years and six and one-half months.[6] After the Tory defeat in 1906, the party leader, Arthur Balfour, lost not only his own constituency seat but most of his Parliamentary support. In 1945, the feeling of most members towards Churchill was one of "special debt to their leader for their very presence in the House: without his 'coat-tail' some must have wondered, how many would have been spared?"[7] This attitude together with the party's soon-to-be realized observation that it was not Churchill, himself, who had brought Conservative fortunes to a low point but the recent history of the Tories with its pre-war record of unemployment[8] strengthened Churchill's ability to shift Conservative energies to a new level of political action.

Winston Churchill's initial reaction was not one of bitterness, resentment or remorse.[9] The direction he chose for the Tories can be discerned as he moved quickly to create the nucleus of his Opposition cadres. He exercised his personal influence through the Conservative Central Office to have Macmillan nominated at the end of August 1945 as the Tory candidate when a vacancy in the solidly middle-class Bromley constituency of North Kent opened when the division's M. P., Sir Edward Campbell, died unexpectedly. When Macmillan was elected, Churchill wrote:

> In the social field at home you are distinguished for your constructive and progressive work. We need you very much on the Opposition Front Bench in the Commons.[10]

To place emphasis on research, policy formulation and political education, Churchill appointed Rab Butler to the chairmanship of the then dormant Conservative Research Department[11] in October of 1945. This was an interesting choice as the Churchill-Butler relationship had earlier been one of an adversarial nature: Butler had backed his party's India policy in the 1930's while Churchill had condemned it; Butler had been a loyal supporter of appeasement, a policy which had kept the Tory rebel Churchill out of power. But during the Second World War, Churchill had named Butler Minister of Education and admired his reformist efforts in passing the 1944 Education Act.[12] He was attracted to Butler's blend of activism and experience, of tradition and open-mindedness. He wanted Butler's Research Department "to produce information and ideas on all the problems likely to arise,"[13] as he perceived the goal of the Research Department as restoring "the whole faih and philosophy of the Conservative Party."[14]

One of the first recruits to this Conservative Research Department was the young ex-soldier, ex-Cambridge graduate, Michael Fraser. The atmosphere of the Conservative Research Department during the Opposition years was one of intellectual excitement, of rubbing shoulders with Churchill, of free debate on issues, of no sacred "political cows."[15] Rab Butler began to refer to this Department as "our Tory neo-Fabians"[16] who continued the search for policy alternatives which the Y.M.C.A. had attempted in the 1920's and 1930's. But unlike the Y.M.C.A., the Conservative Research Department was now placed at the center of the party's re-think, as it had a direct, uncluttered, link to the party's leadership.[17]

Traditionally, the most central of policy organs of the party had been the Shadow Cabinet. Following the General Election and throughout the Opposition era it met every week at 6:00 P. M. on a Wednesday.[18] But, Churchill modified the nature of this group as he avoided appointing Shadow Ministers with exclusive departmental responsibilities. He preferred to give his colleagues the opportunity to attack the government on a wide front. R. A. B. Butler, Harold Macmillan, David Maxwell-Fyfe, and Oliver Lyttelton became the Tory team which dealt with economic and financial questions.[19] Once a fortnight, the members of the Shadow Cabinet, known then as the "Consultative Committee" were given lunch by Churchill in one of the Gilbert and Sullivan rooms of the Savoy Hotel. David Maxwell-Fyfe recalled that it was at these lunches that the "vitality of our leader was nowhere more noticeable than in the food he consumed."[20] During oysters, roast beef, apple tarts, white wine and brandy, Parliamentary strategy was discussed and debating tactics planned. What was emerging was a leadership style devoid of old personalities and policies. Churchill put distance between himself and Beaverbrook, whose "political attitudes were frozen, his ideas were unchanged.... Churchill, on the other hand...was capable of reconsidering even his basic beliefs and throwing up new ideas."[21] The Tory leader also drifted away from the once "faithful Cheetah" of the 1930's and 1940's, Brendan Bracken. While Churchill moved his party away from the slogans of the 1945 election, Bracken returned to the business world by taking over the influential *Financial Times*.[22]

The cessation of political work by the Conservative Party during World War II had resulted in the widespread decay of local Conservative organizations. A most important problem facing Churchill was how to revive these groups not only for the purpose of Parliamentary elections, but also for municipal campaigns.[23] At Churchill's request, Joseph Ball, former chief of the Conservative Research Department, undertook a study of the 1945 General Election.[24] By May 1946, this study was reviewed by Churchill. Its findings were indicative of the state of the party's structure: "the existing machine is quite inadequate to cope with the task which confronts it." A hodgepodge of titles, committees, honorary offices, all working at separate and uncoordinated functions, composed a Conservative Party machine that lacked the ability to tap local talent, let alone organize it.[25] In the area of party advertising, Ball found the Tories fought the 1945 election with a "Publicity Officer" who had "prior to the General Election no experience of organising a national political campaign."[26]

Winston Churchill now faced the issue of who would be named to lead and restructure his party's "grass roots" organization. On May 21, 1946, he wrote to his former Minister of Reconstruction, Lord Woolton.[27] In this letter, Churchill appraised Woolton of the Ball study, that as party leader he accepted its findings, and concluded, "It seems most valuable and I should be glad if you would read it through so that we can discuss it together in the near future."

Attached to this letter was Churchill's own memo, entitled "Brief Summary of the Memorandum: The Last General Election." He stressed the following points:

> Existing Party Organization requires strengthening and re-organising. Chairman of Party—not to be a Member of the House of Commons in order to devote more time to his duties, but should have had political and industrial experience at a high level.[28]

He ended the letter by asking Woolton to think about becoming Chairman of the Conservative Party.

The man who Churchill wanted for party chairman had only joined the Tory Party on the day the 1945 General Election results were made public. Lord Woolton had been a successful retail/advertising executive, yet he was not a Tory die-hard. Educated at Manchester Grammar School and Manchester University, he had participated before the Second World War in the Liverpool University Settlement, a social-action group which dealt with unemployed workers.[29] The scars caused by the hopelessness of urban poverty shaped a social conscience that during World War II produced the White Papers on employment, housing and medical care.[30] After reviewing Churchill's letter and memo, Woolton met with the Tory chief. Lord Woolton recalled:

> Mr. Churchill told me of his concern about the state of the Conservative Party Organization.... He said he believed that nobody else could reorganize the Conservative Party and bring it to a proper state of efficiency and that this view was shared by my friends in the Conservative Shadow Cabinet. He asked me to take the job.[31]

On June 6, 1945, Woolton wrote to Churchill and accepted the party chairmanship, however, he knew that what Churchill wanted was an organization that could function in every ward and precinct.[32] But this was to be no easy task.

Lord Woolton found the Conservative Party organization which he had inherited to be "the most topsy-like arrangement that I had ever come across."[33] Its Central Office had no control over the local constituency associations which at the national level formed a composite National Union of Conservative and Unionist Associasions. The Central Office was not allowed by the local constituency associations to have any influence in the selection of candidates. Lord Woolton claimed that his first inclination was "to come to a sound business conclusion and to tell the Party that the best thing to do with machinery of this nature was to scrap it and start again."[34] However, he soon realized that such independent groupings had grown up around a lot of very hard-working and loyal members. He decided not to scrap, but to keep these various constituency organizations for it was at this level that the Conservative structure would be refashioned. Lord Woolton's basic plan was that every constituency association should be responsible for the organization of a campaign "corp" in each polling district. The fundamental unit of each local corp was to be the "block," which became the responsibility of voluntary workers. By canvassing the block, new members were to be enrolled in a voter registrar, with a notation opposite each voter showing party preference, which became the basis for monitoring voter reaction to Tory election appeals.[35]

Other changes were introduced. A Director of Information Services at the Central Office, London, was appointed to shape Tory advertising programs.[36] Public relations officials or "area information officers" were selected to channel pamphlets, flyers and information bulletins to the local constituency associations.[37] Financial bulletins were circulated to assist constituencies in overcoming difficulties with generally-used methods of fund-raising programs. Other innovations were: the Labour Party was henceforth referred to in Tory literature as the "Socialist" party in an attempt to associate the government "with the Socialist conception that all labour should be employed by the state— a bureaucratic conception lacking in all the warmth that comes from human relationships;"[38] to counter Labourite appeals to youth, the "Young Conservatives" was established and began to attract a body of university students to its ranks. Prior to Woolton's chairmanship, local municipal elections were not contested on a party-name basis by the Tories. This had given the Labour Party a tremendous voter recognition advantage over the Conservative Party because Labourites were elected to local office as organizers of education, local health officials, and those offices that determined the extent of municipal housing or administered transportation, gas, electrical and water services.[39] Lord Woolton changed this election strategy as the Conservatives now would campaign under their party's name for such local positions.

On March 25, 1947, Woolton wrote to Churchill requesting his backing for the union of anti-Socialist associations—Liberal, Nationalist, and Tory in those constituencies where the Conservative Party was the dominant partner. The memo ended, "I shall be grateful to know that this agreement has your approval as Leader of the Party, so that I can subsequently submit it to the Executive Committee of the National Union (Liberals) for their endorsement."[40] Winston Churchill accepted this strategy and on May 8, 1947, an agreement to contest Parliamentary by-elections was reached with the National Liberals by Woolton.[41] These same National Liberals had polled over a million votes in the 1945 General Election. Yet despite Woolton's efforts, general election cooperation with the Liberals failed to materialize in the Opposition Years.

Lord Woolton's biggest gamble as party chairman came in the period March through October 1947 when he publicly challenged the Tories to raise the then staggering amount of one million pounds. Under the heading, "Lord Woolton's Fighting Fund," he sought to arouse national voter attention, inject the party structure with much needed funds, and showcase a new Conservative image as a reformed, modern party:

> Everyone thinks of it (Tory Party) as a rich party...and our opponents always try to make out that we are a rich man's party. Neither is true.... I want money, then, to prepare for the great

fight for liberty which is ahead—the next General Election.... We can't afford only to draw candidates from the people with money. We don't want to do so. It would be wrong; we are a democratic party. We come from all classes of society and so must our candidates. It is ability and character that we want.[42]

Although the results of this appeal would not be known until 1948, the effect of Woolton's organizational efforts first became apparent in the municipal elections of November 1947. The Conservatives won 636 seats and lost only 18, while the ruling Labour Party contested 730 local offices, winning in 43 but losing in 687. Most noticeable was the shift to the Conservative Party in the industrial areas of North-West England.[43]

Political scientist Richard Rose has observed that a crucial problem facing a British opposition leader is that his activities can be so concentrated on the immediate effort of securing public awareness of the failures of a ruling government that the "future can be reckoned to look after itself." Thus, if broad policy has not been formulated "prior to entering office, the [opposition leader and his party] are unlikely to have time to do so in office."[44] Winston Churchill's opposition strategy sought to avoid this pitfall. The process began at the Conservative Party Conference at Blackpool on October 5, 1946. Here the Party Leader set the direction for policy formulation:

Our Conservative aim is to build...a property-owning democracy, both independent and interdependent. In this I include profit-sharing schemes in suitable industries and intimate consultation between employers and wage-earners. In fact, we seek so far as possible to make the status of the wage-earner that of a partner in industry or business rather than of an irresponsible employee. We are now moving forward into another vast scheme of National Insurance, which arose, even in the stress of war, from a Parliament with a great Conservative majority. It is an essential principle...Tory policy...to defend the general public against abuses by monopolies and against restraints on trade and enterprises, whether these evils come from private corporations...or from the incompetence and arbitrariness of Departments of State. Finally, we declare ourselves the unsleeping opponents of all class, all official or all Party privilege....[45]

Following this speech, Churchill created an "Industrial Policy Committee" or IPC, which he asked to formulate a new Conservative economic policy.[46] Chosen as committee members were: Butler (Chairman), Macmillan, David Maxwell-Fyfe, Oliver Lyttelton, and Michael Fraser of the Conservative Research Department. The committee was to complete its work by April 1947 and report its findings to the next party conference at Brighton in October 1947.[47]

Rab Butler moved quickly and on October 29, 1946, he circulated a memorandum to his colleagues proposing five areas of study: Worker in Industry, Monopoly, Nationalised Industries and their Future, Exports, and Government and Industry.[48] The committee was to have at its disposal the staff of the Conservative Research Department, which now included Reginald Maulding and David Clarke, who had been assisting Shadow Cabinet members in preparing their Parliamentary speeches.[49] The IPC's first meeting took place in Room F, House of Commons, on November 5, 1946.[50] Hugh Berrington has written that issues of an ideological nature play little part in Tory disputes.[51] This was true of the IPC as pragmatic policies dealing with Butler's five areas emerged as the committee's objectives.

Nationalization was not to be opposed on the basis of vague "free enterprise" slogans, for the committee felt it would not "be practicable to give a conclusive answer until we have seen not merely some of the nationalization legislation but also nationalization in practice."[52] At this November meeting it was agreed that the IPC should produce a general statement covering industrial policy and industrial relations which would be concise in style and contemporary in substance. Harold Macmillan was asked to prepare the first draft.[53] By November 25, 1946, he had produced "Government and Industry." It advocated:

No Government of whatever complexion can disassociate itself from a large degree of intervention and indeed management of the economic life of a modern state.... The question is not whether the government should play a part in the industrial and economic life of the country. The question is by what means and at what level and for what purpose. A compromise must therefore be devised between the extreme individualism of the early 19th Century and the totalitarian tendencies of Modern Socialism.[54]

Building on the arguments of the earlier work, *Industry and the State*, Macmillan advanced the idea that the center of postwar Conservative thought should be the implementation of a mixed economy of free enterprise and collectivist approaches.

At the November 29th meeting of the IPC, a decision was reached that its members would next contact the local constituency associations and discuss with industrialists and trade unionists their reactions to this kind of postwar Conservative thought.[55] It was also decided that the final product of the IPC would be divided into three sections—an introduction, a part dealing with government and industry, and a section concerned with workers. By December 5, 1946, Macmillan first used the term "a new Industrial Charter" in another draft paper that proposed the introduction of a legislative program to provide that in businesses employing more than fifty workers a "consultative council or works council" should be established which would create a worker-management code of conduct for its business.[56]

On January 27, 1947, papers on the coal industry, civil aviation, transportation, monopoly and employment were finalized. The IPC's effort was put in document form under the title, "Industrial Charter," which was written by David Clarke and Michael Fraser.[57] While condemning monopolies and a lack of adequate housing then being constructed by the Labour Government, the "Industrial Charter" addressed itself to two broad groups:

To the worker, we offer a new charter giving assurance of steady employment, incentives to test his ability to the utmost and status as an individual personality. To the consumer we offer the ultimate restoration of freedom of choice, the prospect of a better standard of living and protection from restrictive practices.[58]

Asking the question: "Can mass unemployment, the memory of which has scarred the minds of millions of British men and women, be banished by a modern industrial and financial policy?,"[59] the "Industrial Charter" stated that the maintenance of "employment will be among the most important subjects under constant review"[60] by any future Conservative government. A "Workers Charter" comprised the section on Conservative relations with the trade union movement. It spoke of establishing Macmillan's co-partnership councils in British industries to upgrade the status of the worker and to make the worker more of a participant in his industrial environment. Furthermore, reductions in income tax levels, support for collective bargaining and for such social services as universal health care, old age pensions and allowances for large families were listed as basic Conservative policy.

After the document was finalized, the "Industrial Charter" was sent to Churchill. Harold Macmillan "was surprised at the attention he gave, not merely, as one might expect, to the drafting but to the substance."[61] What appealed to Churchill was the shift in direction the "Industrial Charter" sought— one that spoke for a less privileged, more open society.[62] The increased role of the state and the improved status of the worker would help his party dissociate itself "from the immediate past and...was reverting to the Toryism of Lord Randolph Churchill whose son was reviving a belief in Tory democracy."[63] Winston Churchill then approved the "Charter" and it was published in May 1947. Newspaper reactions to the "Charter" among London newspapers paralleled party lines, that is, *Daily Herald* critical, *Daily Mail* full of praise. The response throughout the rest of Britain was much more favorable: the *Yorkshire Post* greeted the "Charter" with marked enthusiasm, calling it "A Better Plan for Every Man"[64] and the liberal *Manchester Guardian* found it a "courageous departure from past Tory pronouncement."[65] The "Industrial Charter's" reception by the fortnightly *Spectator* claimed "it remove[d] the last excuse for labelling the Conservative Party as is presently constituted as reactionary."[66] Lord Beaverbrook's papers (*Daily Express* and *Evening Standard*) mounted the most vociferous attack on the "Industrial Charter" and the IPC.[67] Charges of crypto-socialism were directed at Harold Macmillan, as it had been Macmillan's role to serve as the main spokesperson for the "Charter" prior to Churchill's official recognition of the document at the Brighton Party Conference in October 1947. On June 14, 1947, Macmillan countered the attacks from the Right in these words:

> The Industrial Charter is merely a restatement in the light of modern conditions of the fundamental and lasting principles of our Party.... So all the forces of reaction in the country [including] Lord Beaverbrook...are united in saying that this Industrial Charter is not Tory policy. What they really mean, all of them, is that they wish it were not Tory policy. Fortunately, their wishes cannot be granted. In any case, important as our critics may be, I prefer to rest upon the tradition of Disraeli, fortified by the high authority of Churchill.[68]

At the Brighton Conference in October, the resolution requesting the acceptance of the "Charter" was unanimously accepted.[69] Winston Churchill's conference speech of October 4, 1947, was symbolic of the new direction of the Conservative Party. His remarks dealt with concrete domestic issues:

> There is a legend which is spread about—that the Conservative Party is not concerned about the sufferings arising from unemployment, that they are callous about the problems and agony of a man who wishes to work and cannot find a job.[70]

He then told his audience this "legend" could best be countered by looking to Conservatism's progressive tradition—of the support given to the workers' right to organize by Benjamin Disraeli and his Tory administrations, of Lord Woolton's efforts as Minister of Reconstruction in Churchill's wartime government and presently that in "our

Industrial Charter, which is the official policy of the party, we have shown quite plainly the broad democratic view we take of current affairs and the many forms of social activity which we expose and encourage in our...progressive Party."[71] He reminded his listeners that his party's new Conservatism now supported an industrial philosophy that had cut its ties from the idea of industry being divided into two sides. The "Charter" wanted to promote a new spirit of involvement in the workplace through joint consultation, work committees and co-partnership schemes. The Tories intended to reconcile individual effort with a proper measure of central planning in order to free private endeavor from the taint of selfishness or class privilege.

The progressive Toryism that Churchill advanced for his party was not welcomed by the Tory Right. Writing to Lord Beaverbrook at the conclusion of the Brighton Conference on October 7, 1947, Brendan Bracken spoke of the "neo-socialists, like Harold Macmillan, who are in favour of nationalizing railways, electricity, gas and many other things."[72] Disappointed with Churchill's leadership, Bracken ended his letter, "I know not whether the Tories' return to their ancient faith is likely to get us more votes. It certainly won't lose us any."[73] But the "ancient faith" that Churchill looked to was a Conservatism which called for: stimulating industrial efficiency by means of government assisted research programs which would make such efforts more readily available to small and medium-size firms' and an empirical approach to nationalization. It would be this kind of doctrine that was to serve as Churchill's guide when he addressed, in Parliament, the actions of the Labour Government of Clement Attlee.

Notes

[1] Harold Mcmillan, *Tides of Fortune, 1945-1955*, p. 33.

[2] Earl of Kilmuir, *Political Adventure, The Memoirs of the Earl of Kilmuir* (London: Weidenfield and Nicolson, 1964), p. 136.

[3]Ibid., P. 137.

[4]Early Selbourne Papers, Letter of July 30, 1945, Earl of Selbourne to Winston S. Churchill (Bodleian Library, Oxford University).

[5]J. F. S. Ross, *Parliamentary Representation*, p. 247.

[6]Ibid.

[7]J. D. Hoffman, *The Conservative Party in Opposition 1945-1951* (London: McGibbon and Kee, 1964), p. 48.

[8]Butler Papers, RAB, G17, 1-243, 1945 Notes, July 1945, "Reflections on the Recent Election," (Trinity College, Cambridge).

[9]Great Britain, Parliament, *Parliamentary Debates* (Commons), 5th Series, 413 (1945): 86.

[10]Nigel Fisher, *Harold Macmillan*, p. 122; see also, Alistair Horne, *Harold Macmillan*, Vol. I, *1894-1956* (New York: Viking Penguin Inc. 1989), p. 287.

[11]Butler Papers, RAB, H, 46, "The Conservative Research Department and Conservative Recovery After 1945," Memorandum, Michael Fraser to Mr. Butler, September 6, 1961 (Trinity College, Cambridge University).

[12]John Colville, *Winston Churchill and His Inner Circle*, p. 236.

[13]Earl of Kilmuir, *Political Adventure*, p. 147.

[14]Conservative Research Department Files, "ACP Correspondence, 1949-1951," (Bodleian Library, Oxford University).

[15]Interview, Lord Fraser of Kilmorack, London, England, House of Lords, July 24, 1986.

[16]R. A. Butler, "A Disraelian Approach to Modern Politics." in *Tradition and Change: Nine Oxford Lectures*, by R. A. Butler, et al. (London: Conservative Political Centre, 1954), p. 10.

[17]John Ramsden, *The Making of Conservative Party Policy, The Conservative Research Department Since 1929* (London, Longman, 1980), p. 9.

[18]Earl of Kilmuir, *Political Adventure*, p. 149.

[19]Fisher, *Harold Macmillan*, p. 123.

[20]Earl of Kilmuir, *Political Adventure*, p. 149.

[21]Young, *Churchill and Beaverbrook*, p. 272.

[22]Charles Edward Lysaght, *Brendan Bracken*(London: Allen Lane, 1979), p. 256.

[23]Butler Papers, RAB, G17, 1-243, 1945, Notes, July 1945, "Reflections on the Recent Election," (Trinity College, Cambridge University).

[24]Woolton Papers, M. S. Woolton, 21, Correspondence as Chairman, Conservative Party, June 1945-March 1955 (Bodleian Library, Oxford University).

[25]Ibid., p. 1.

[26]Ibid., p. 3.

[27]Woolton Papers, M. S. Woolton, 21, Correspondence as Chairman, Conservative Party, Letter, Winston S. Churchill to Lord Woolton, May 21, 1946 (Bodleian Library, Oxford University).

[28]Woolton Papers, M. S. Woolton, 21, Correspondence as Chairman, Conservative Party, Memo by Winston Churchill, "Brief Summary of Last General Election," May 21, 1946 (Bodleian Library, Oxford University).

[29]Conservative Party Papers, Historical Manuscripts, Report on the Correspondence and Papers of Frederick James Marques, 1st Earl of Woolton, p. 2 (Bodleian Library, Oxford University).

[30]Ibid., pp. 5-6.

[31]Earl of Woolton, *Memoirs*, p. 328.

[32]Woolton Papers, M. S. Woolton, 21, Correspondence as Chairman, Conservative Party, June 1945-March 1955, Letter, Winston S. Churchill to Lord Woolton, November 3, 1947 (Bodleian Library, Oxford).

[33]Earl of Woolton, *Memoirs*, p. 331.

[34]Ibid., P. 332.

[35]Ibid., p. 341.

[36]68th Annual Conference Report of the Conservative Party, 1947, p. 20.

[37]J. D. Hoffman, *The Conservative Party in Opposition 1945-1951*, p. 85.

[38]Earl of Woolton, *Memoirs*, p. 335.

[39]Ibid., p. 340.

[40]Woolton Papers, M. S. Woolton, 21, Correspondence as Chairman, Conservative Party, June 1945-March 1955, Memorandum, Lord Woolton to Winston S. Churchill, March 25, 1947 (Bodleian Library, Oxford University).

[41]Woolton Papers, M. S. Woolton, 21, Agreement of May 8, 1947 (Bodleian Library, Oxford University).

[42]Conservative Party Files, CC04/2/98, Lord Woolton's fighting Fund 1947-1948, pp. 1-2 (Bodleian Library, Oxford University).

[43]Earl of Kilmuir, *Political Adventure*, p, 153.

[44]Richard Rose, "The Variability of Party Government," *Political Studies* 18 (1969): 429.

[45]*Conservatism, 1945-1950*, Conservative Political Centre, London, 1950, pp. 82-83.

[46]Butler Papers, RAB, H. 46, "The Conservative Research Department and Conservative Recovery After 1945," Memorandum, Michael Fraser to Mr. Butler, September 6, 1961, Part III, p. 1 (Trinity College, Cambridge University).

[47]Ibid., p. 2.

[48]Conservative Research File, B/1/w/1 (Bodleian Library, Oxford University).

[49]Ibid.

[50]Ibid.

[51]Hugh Berrington, "Conservative Party," *Political Quarterly* 32 (1961): 373.

[52]Conservative Research File, B/1/w/1 (Bodleian Library, Oxford University).

[53]Ibid.

[54]Ibid.

[55]Ibid.

[56]Conservative Research File, B/1/w/1, Macmillan Draft (Bodleian Library, Oxford University).

[57]Butler Papers, RAB, H 46, "The Conservative Research Department and Conservative Recovery After 1945," Memorandum, Michael Fraser to Mr. Butler, September 6, 1961, p. 4.

[58]"Industrial Charter," in *Conservatism, 1945-1950*, Conservative Political Centre, London, 1950, p. 51.

[59]Ibid., p. 59.

[60]Ibid.

[61]Macmillan, *Tides of Fortune*, p. 302.

[62]Interview, Sir John Colville, London, England, July 16, 1986.

[63]Earl of Woolton, *Memoirs*, 359; see also, Macmillan, *Tides of Fortune*, p. 308.

[64]*Yorkshire Post*, "A Better Plan for Every Man," May 12, 1947.

[65]*Manchester Guardian*, "The New Toryism", May 12, 1947.

[66]*Spectator*, "Tory Programme," May 16, 1947.

[67]*Daily Express*, "Under Which Flag," May 12, 1947; *Evening Standard*, "Change of Heart," May 12, 1947.

[68]Macmillan, *Tides of Fortune*, p. 306.

[69]68th Annual Conference Report of the Conservative Party, 1947, p. 37.

[70]Robert Rhodes James, ed., *Winston S. Churchill, His Complete Speeches, 1897-1963*, Vol. VII, (1943-1944), p. 7530.

[71]Ibid. p. 7534.

[72]Brendan Bracken Papers, Letter, Bracken to Lord Beaverbrook, October 7, 1947 (Churchill College, Cambridge).

[73]Ibid.

CHAPTER V

CHURCHILL IN OPPOSITION

"The whole enterprise, initiative, contrivance and genius of the British nation is being increasingly paralysed by the restrictions which are imposed upon it in the name of a mistaken political philosophy and a largely obsolete mode of thought."

Winston S. Churchill
House of Commons
October 28, 1947.

The solitary struggle against a triumphant Germany and the subsequent partnership with the United States had raised British influence in the world to a level which could not be sustained. The underlying weakness of the English economy was concealed in the euphoria of victory. After the extraordinary exertions the nation had made during the war, Britain was bankrupt for the first time in its history. It could not pay its debts or even pay its way without further borrowing from the United States.

The war had cost Britain a quarter of her national wealth, a large portion of which was accounted for by the destruction of physical assets such as housing, but the most important item in this inventory was the loss of foreign assets valued at 4,200 million pounds to pay for supplies purchased abroad during the war. The earnings on these foreign assets had played a big part in paying for British imports before the war. Now, simply to pay for the pre-war level of imports, which included much of its food and raw materials for industry, Britain would have to increase exports by fifty to seventy-five percent over pre-war figures, and this at a time when the pent-up demand at home was quite capable of absorbing everything that a rundown British industry, still turning back from war production, could hope to supply.

The Labour Government of 1945 was committed to programs of nationalization without having given much thought to the way in which nationalized industries should operate. As the Minister of Fuel and Power stated at the end of 1947, "There was far too little detailed preparation in the formulation of schemes of nationalization and in consequence we found ourselves with legislation that had to be completed without the necessary blueprints."[1] The government wished to embark upon expensive social welfare programs, whose costs were undefined. Likewise, it had little idea of what to do about inflation and was not conscious of succeeding to the management of a bankrupt economy critically dependent on what it could buy and borrow from other nations. While the war had provided a valuable education in management, it was management of a war economy with little foretaste of the problems of peace. Still, the slogans of an earlier and very different decade continued to reverberate in ministers' speeches and thinking as their emphasis was on the need to retain controls in order to insure a society of fair shares. It was distribution, not production, that was uppermost in their minds. Also, the Labour Government did not clarify whether there were some fixed objectives for particular industries, which economists refer to as "aggregates," that is, the volume of investment, to which everything else should be subordinated and upheld even if circumstances were radically altered by events.

Thus, the details of organizational structure, finance, the compensation of private stockholders affected by nationalization schemes, pricing policy, or the system of consultation with industrial workers was left extremely vague. As one of Labour's powerful spokesmen, Secretary of the TUC and head of the controlling board of the nationalized electrical industries, Walter Citrine, admitted— the method by which industries were to be taken into public ownership "had not been thought out with any precision."[2]

For the leader of a victorious party, Attlee was remarkably lacking in any charismatic quality and showed little interest in ideas. In Cabinet, he behaved more like the impartial chairman of a committee than the leader of a government.[3] Nor "did he supply any new initiatives in policy in most areas; in economic matters he seemed particularly at a loss."[4] His Cabinet of twenty was much larger than the wartime cabinets of five to nine members. Even so, a number of important peacetime ministers were excluded, such as Food, Supply and Transport. He created a record 157 standing committees and 306 *ad hoc* committees.[5] There was no more towering figure on the industrial front than the Labourite leader, Ernest Bevin, yet Attlee channelled Bevin's considerable energies into foreign relations as Foreign Secretary.

Hugh Dalton, who had hoped to serve at the foreign office became, instead, Chancellor of the Exchequer. But the key economic position was given to Herbert Morrison, who as Lord President of the Council, presided over the standing committee on the home front to deal with economic planning. However, Morrison's career had been made in "local government on a metropolitan scale. As Minister of Transport in the brief Labour Administration [of Ramsey MacDonald] he had been the real creator of the unified London Transport System."[6] This skillful master of Labour's party machine and organizer of the General Election victory now had to deal with a wide assortment of domestic policy problems. The chief defect of this machinery was that given Morrison's responsibilities with the nationalization programs, which the government intended to pass within a short period, the time necessary for economic planning became less and less. As a consequence, fiscal policy was not linked to economic policy when it lay increasingly at the heart of economic planning.[7] The demands placed on Morrison also meant that neither fiscal nor monetary policy emerged as important ingredients in Labour's economic programs.[8]

The most urgent problem facing the new Labour Government in August of 1945 was the financing of a large and unavoidable external debt. When American Lend-Lease ended, Britain's deficit was 1,200 million pounds a year.[9] Such a burden could only be met by a loan and only the United States could provide such funds. The Prime Minister dispatched John Maynard Keynes to Washington, D. C. to negotiate an agreement. Prior to the end of the war, Keynes had predicted the need for such funds and had been optimistic that the United States would be a willing and eager source of either a grant or interest-free loan.[10] But between the time Keynes had written his early analysis in January of 1945 and his departure date of September 13, 1945, policies were made by men who were largely unfamiliar with each other.

The American Congress began to take a harder look at voting for "foreign aid" to those countries that sought to nationalize or socialize industry.[11] In lieu of these changes, the new Chancellor of the Exchequer found Keynes "almost starry-eyed. He was confident that in the coming negotiations he could obtain American aid that would be ample in amount and in most satisfactory conditions. He told us [the Cabinet] that he thought he could get 1,500 million pounds ($6 billion) as a free gift or 'grant' in-aid. There would be no question of a loan to be repaid, or a rate of interest on the loan."[12] But Keynes thinking proved unrealistic. The Americans were dead against a grant or interest-free loan. On December 6, 1945, a loan figure was agreed upon: $3.75 billion, at two percent interest, with repayment over a fifty year period. However, under pressure from the Americans, Keynes and his negotiating team had to agree that the pound would be made freely convertible into dollars within eighteen months of the agreement, and that imperial preference (tariffs against U.S. goods) would be abolished. Given England's need for external cash, the Labour Cabinet accepted such terms, but the problem was that Great Britain was running a deficit of goods imported to goods exported to the United States. Also, England lacked an adequate compensating inflow of dollars from its accounts with other countries. It was asking much of the weakened British economy to make its currency convertible, that is, as acceptable as the dollar. Not only were dollars scarcer in the postwar world, sterling was abundant. England, to all appearances, was now holding itself out as a bridge between the dollar and other currencies when it lacked the necessary strength.

Except for a brief period in the 1920's, the Tory Party, unlike its leader, had not experienced Opposition politics from 1923 to 1945.[13] Winston Churchill knew that Labour had a two to one majority in the 1945 Parliament, which meant that a strategy of simply "opposing for opposing sake" would be futile. Also, many of the domestic bills introduced in the August 16, 1945 session calling for the nationalization of the Bank of England, civil aviation, wireless and coal mines were not opposed since these industries had been controlled by the Coalition Government during World War II. Furthermore, Churchill had already stated that these industries would best be left under state control during the General Election campaign.[14] The early outline of his party's Parliamentary strategy came in the debate on the King's Address on August 16, 1945:

> Allowance must also be made for the transitional period through which we are passing.... The same is true of the proposal to nationalize the coalmines if that is really the best way of securing a larger supply of coal at a cheaper price. I for one should approach the plan in a sympathetic spirit. It is by results...that the Government will be judged, and it is by results that this policy must be judged.[15]

His pragmatic style stressed that a major difference between Tory and Labour economic doctrines would be the importance the Tories placed on production. Britain's postwar economy could only pay for the social welfare schemes called for by both the Coalition and Labour Governments not by heavy taxation: "the entire area has been swept through, harvested and gleaned...a thoroughly scrubbed field,"[16] not by retaining or increasing controls on British industry: "industry and enterprise are fettered, hampered and hobbled by an ever-spreading network of controls and regulations,"[17] but by policies whereby state intervention assisted postwar investment and production through selective grants to those industries which were capable of providing the greatest catalyst for industrial recovery.

By December 1945, Churchill made the housing industry the lynch pin of how the Tories judged Labour economic policy.[18] By criticizing Housing Minister Aneurin Bevan's procedure whereby departmentally approved licenses became necessary for construction companies and local municipalities to implement housing starts, the Conservative sought to deflate Labour's election slogans.[19]

Also, Churchill's criticism of the American loan was aimed at the convertibility provision of the agreement "this convertibility proposal within 15 months appears to be a proposition so doubtful and perilous."[20] He believed that not enough thought had been given to Britain's ability to underwrite the world's dollar shortage that was impacting on trade and finance in the postwar years. The Tory leader asked: could the English economy realistically settle accounts with the United States dollar, now demanded by virtually all countries outside North America? Would not such a plan adversely affect Britain's postwar industrial production? What if those nations draw on the existing holdings of sterling for conversion into dollars because the dollar seemed more likely to hold its value or because the dollar was needed to finance current purchases?

Of all the shortages constraining government policy in the 1945-1951 period, the shortage of energy and particularly of coal was among the most damaging. What gave cause for concern was the low level and downward trend of coal production over and against the expansion in domestic requirements as industrial output increased. There was also an urgent need to resume exports of coal to earn much-needed foreign exchange. Likewise, recovery of coal production might prove the key to the dollar shortage problem by providing alternative sources of supply for a wide-range of imports. The bottleneck came when the Minister of Fuel and Power, Emmanuel Shinwell, who was given jurisdiction over coal production, could not recruit enough manpower to increase coal production. Yet, following Shinwell's lead, his ministry claimed on October 12, 1946 that "more labour was not needed in [the coal] industry."[21] The situation was brought to crisis proportions when in December of 1946 and January of 1947, England experienced the most severe spell of icy weather of the century. Although Shinwell in his autobiography claims problems of transportation caused what proved to be Britain's first major economic dislocation,[22] on February 7, 1947, he told a shocked Cabinet that the House of Commons would have to be informed that all electricity must be cut off from industry for five hours a day throughout London, South-East England, the Midlands and North-West sections of the nation as well as from all domestic consumers.[23] Clement Attlee responded in a public broadcast of February 17, 1947, by expressing "confidence that the [fuel shortage] would be overcome and the economic and social life of the country brought to a new level of prosperity."[24] Yet, for the first time in its industrial history, British industrial production was effectively stopped for three weeks— something German bombing had never been able to do. Registered unemployment rose from under 400,000 to over 2.3 million.[25]

Winston Churchill used this crisis to indict the Labour Government for a lack of efficient and effective planning, thus introducing a new theme into his style of opposition tactics—equating socialism with mismanagement. While debating Shinwell, he claimed:

> The gravamen of the charge the right hon. Gentleman [Shinwell] has to meet is not the general difficulties of the coal situation but his precise conduct in not having a practical plan for dealing with the electricity supplies of the country when a serious emergency arose.[26]

He expressed Tory concern for the hardship such a crisis placed on wage earners[27] while associating his party with the hopes of the postwar generation:

> There was a widespread belief a year and a half ago, or even a year ago, that some quite definite reward in the shape of a mitigation of basic conditions would come to our people as a consequence of victory...in spite of all the expectations which were dangled before them, vaunted before them—all the which were held out—is a deep and bitter disappointment. I am not going to put all the blame upon the Minister of Fuel and Power.... The cause of our troubles is wider and deeper than the shortcomings or foolish speeches or contradictory forecasts of any Minister.[28]

The "cause" was Socialist mismanagement[29] which had added 1,007,000 civil servants to the bureaucracy of committees, sub-committees and departments but failed to create adequate administrative plans to effectively ration Britain's fuel supplies.[30]

On July 15, 1947, the provision for full convertibility under the American loan went into effect. Attlee's Chancellor of the Exchequer told the House that Conservative fears "of England's ability to handle the convertibility provision of the Anglo-American Loan Agreement were misplaced."[31] This statement reflected a widespread government optimism that "the fateful day [has] brought with it no consequential disaster, nor is any in sight."[32] The *Manchester Guardian* spoke of "some extra drain [which] is unlikely to be very large," while the *Economist* mentioned the "probably small additional cost of convertibility."[33] But by August 11, 1947, the Prime Minister was stating that England was facing an economic crisis "as serious as any that had faced us in our long history."[34]

On August 21, 1947, Chancellor Dalton reported dollar loan losses of $66,000 in a two-day period on top of a $176,000,000 reduction in dollar reserves during the week preceding August 21st.[35] In a memo to the Cabinet, Dalton claimed that England was racing through its United States dollar loan credit at such a speed that if cuts in imports, increased food rationing and a suspension of convertibility were not undertaken, the entire United States loan would be used up by June of 1948.[36] What had happened? A combination of factors caused this situation. The February coal crisis had cost foreign exchange in the form of reduced exports. This had increased speculative efforts to sell sterling as holders of pounds sought the security of the stronger dollar. Those scarce dollars held by England were being spent on American imports, as the Labour Government remained more dependent than had been foreseen on American supplies. In addition, scarce dollars had been used to feed those Germans living in the British zone of occupation: $60 million alone in the first three months of 1947,[37] and after the fusion of the British and American zone, England had even to pay for the American share of food supplies as well as its own.[38]

A *Manchester Guardian* article of July 25, 1947, compared the financial crisis with that of 1931 when MacDonald's Labour Administration collapsed.[39] Alan Bullock, Ernest Bevin's biographer, wrote in his concluding volume that this crisis led both Morrison and Dalton to initiate talks for the removal of Attlee as Prime Minister.[40] This kind of bickering presented the picture of an uncertain, drifting government. By September 30, 1947, Attlee appointed Sir Stafford Cripps to head a new Department of Economic Affairs which superseded Morrison's Lord President's Committee.[41] By November 14, 1947, Attlee had replaced Dalton as Chancellor with Cripps.[42] A new policy of austerity was introduced which included cuts in food imports, increases in exports and sharp reductions in consumer purchasing power through sales and profit taxes—all this done in the hope of stabilizing the dollar drain.[43] To implement its new economic plans the Labour Government wanted to extend the legislative life of a 1945 wartime "Defense Regulations Act" that would allow the government to regulate the economy without prior Parliamentary approval. As Morrison told the House of Commons: "If it is to be argued that every time the Government wishes to do something which is urgent in this economic field, we have to bring in a separate Bill, that seems to be making completely foolish all the talk about the critical situation in which the country finds itself at the present time."[44]

Labour's response to both coal and convertibility developments presented Churchill with the opportunity to: (1) equate Tory actions with traditional British liberties; (2) reinforce his argument that socialist planning leads to administrative inefficiencies; and (3) differentiate Conservative policy from Socialist programs and philosophy. He undertook this effort during the Parliamentary sessions of August 8, 1947 and August 11, 1947. Initially, he stated that the economic crisis was partly "due to the inevitable conditions of the aftermath of so great a war, in which we made such immense exertions."[45] Yet, even when such allowances were made and support given to the government to restore Britain's economic position, to respond to the crisis by acquiesing in Morrison's request would be to give "a blank cheque"[46] that would be "the negation of British freedom and our way of life in time of peace."[47] He reinforced his argument by mentioning that it would be the workers who would suffer "the menace of uncertainty"[48] from such a change in the law as they would be at the mercy of administrative orders to work or not to work in selected industries, if such was mandated under the proposed law. He adroitly associated the Tory Party with the cause of ancient political freedoms:

The point is that the Government is taking away from the legislative and parliamentary instrument the duties which it ought to discharge and taking to themselves, without precise or preconceived plan, vast powers which sweep away all the liberties which we have hitherto enjoyed.[49]

By the end of August 1947 Churchill asked for and was given a review of the Labour's economic policy by Oliver Lyttelton.[50] With the help of this information, he debated government domestic policy on the sixth day of debate on the King's Speech on Octber 28, 1947. The failure to supply Britain with enough energy and the collapse of the nation's financial reserves was caused by the failure of Socialist planning. Productivity was weakened by nationalization.[51] The Tories would support Cripps' plan to increase exports but his call to reduce food imports and ration consumer goods was said to demonstrate the major difference between Labour and Conservative domestic policy: "The conception that any community can make its living without a healthy and vigorous home market and strong domestic consuming power is a fallacy."[52] He then identified the Labour Party as one which was wedded to old "shibboleths"[53] of economic thought, and mentioned for the first time a phrase that was later to become a Tory election motto: "set the people free."[54] The term was used in connection with his criticism of Labour's philosophy of government: "The whole enterprise, initiative, contrivance and genius of the British nation is being increasingly paralysed by the restrictions which are imposed upon it in the name of a mistaken political philosophy and a largely obsolete mode of thought."[55]

Churchill then spoke of Labour's "incompetence in administration"[56] that hampered the housing industry. The Tory leader mentioned an enormous number of people crowded into substandard housing owing to a government policy that favored the building of municipal flats or apartments over private residences.[57] The total number of new homes now projected to be built in England by 1949 "in the fifth year after the war was over is to be no more than

140,000 houses.... One hundred and forty thousand houses in 1949, in spite of our bitter need, and under the Socialist Government. That compares with 350,000 houses built in the year before the war...under a Tory Government."[58] It is interesting to observe that Labour's response to Churchill's critique was not addressed to the general thrust of his arguments—inefficiency, limits on personal freedom, lack of productivity, but consisted on the Lord President's recital of the economic problems of the 1930's, allegedly caused by a lack of planning.[59]

As 1947 gave way to 1948, what can one conclude in terms of the direction that Churchill gave to his party?

1. Winston Churchill's ideas were beginning to generate a more favorable image for the Tories. The Gallup Poll published in the *News Chronicle* in August 1947 found that, for the first time since the General Election, the Conservative Party had overtaken the Labour Party by 44.5 percent to 41 percent in voter preference.

2. This favorable image was also reflected by the high Tory vote in the November 1947 municipal elections.

3. At Churchill's request, an *Industrial Charter* had been produced which was the "the first landmark on the road to Conservative recovery in the field of ideas."[61]

4. He had appointed a new party chairman who was beginning to remold and remodel the party's structure which had contributed to the surprising 1947 municipal elections results.

5. Butler had been given full authority to develop a research organization that dedicated its efforts to the pursuit of contemporary approaches to government services.

6. Churchill's Parliamentary rhetoric had paralleled the new postwar Conservative thought and projected Tory policy as one concerned with the need for managing an efficient but humane economy.

7. A younger generation of Tories, such as Macmillan, Butler and Fraser had been empowered to generate new

domestic formulas and question old Tory tenets. Their activities had been endorsed by the party leader.

8. Clementine Churchill's remark that the 1945 General Election defeat was a "blessing in disguise" had a ring of truth to it. The party had not been out of power for almost thirty years. It had not examined its philosophy or programs.[62] Turned out of office by this stunning electoral rebuff, the Conservatives now sought novel approaches to postwar political, social, and economic developments.

Notes

[1]Sir Norman Chester, *The Nationalisation of British Industry, 1945-1951* (London: His Majesty's Stationary Office, 1975), p. 1008.

[2]Lord Citrine, *Two Careers* (London: Hutchinson, 1967), p. 263.

[3]Alan Bullock, *Ernest Bevin, Foreign Secretary, 1945-1951* (New York: W. W. Norton and Company, 1983), p. 55

[4]Kenneth O. Morgan, *Labour in Power, 1945-1951* (Oxford: Clarendon Press, 1984), p. 48.

[5]Ibid., p. 49.

[6]Lord Salter, *Memoirs of a Public Servant* (London: Faber and Faber, 1961), p. 287.

[7]Alec Cairncross, *Years of Recovery, British Economic Policy, 1945-1951* (London: Methuen, 1985), p. 51.

[8]Ibid., p. 52.

[9]Great Britain, Parliament, *Parliamentary Debates* (Commons), 5th Series, 413 (August 24, 1945): 956.

[10]Letter, Keynes to F. G. Lee, January 23, 1945, in *The Collected Writings of John Maynard Keynes* (ed. D. Mayridge, Vol. 24 (Cambridge, University Press for Royal Economic Society, 1979), p. 251.

[11]Richard N. Gardner, *Sterling-Dollar Diplomacy* (Oxford: University Press, 1956), p. 194.

[12]Lord Dalton (Hugh Dalton), *High Tide and After* (London: Frederick Muller, 1962), p. 73.

[13]Interview, Lord Fraser of Kilmorack, London, England, House of Lords, July 24, 1986.

[14]Woolton Papers, M. S. Woolton, 21, Correspondence as Chairman Conservative Party, Letter, Winston S. Churchill to Lord Woolton, June 6, 1945 (Bodleian Library, Oxford University).

[15]Great Britain, Parliament, *Parliamentary Debates* (Commons), 5th Series, 413 (August 16, 1945): 93-94.

[16]Great Britain, Parliament, *Parliamentary Debates* (Commons), 5th Series, 414 (October 23, 1945): 1408

[17]Great Britain, Parliament, *Parliamentary Debates* (Commons), 5th Series, 416 (December 6, 1945): 2536.

[18]Ibid., p. 2542.

[19]Ibid.

[20]Great Britain, Parliament, *Parliamentary Debates* (Commons), 5th Series, 417 (December 13, 1946):714

[21]*The Economist*, October 12, 1946.

[22]Lord Shinwell, *Conflict Without Malice* (London: Odhams Press, 1955), pp. 180-185.

[23]Lord Dalton, *High Tide and After*, pp. 203-204.

[24]Attlee Papers, M. S. 131, 1937-1947 (Bodleian Library, Oxford University).

[25]Cairncross, *Years of Recovery, British Economic Policy, 1945-1951*, p. 366.

[26]Great Britain, Parliament, *Parliamentary Debates* (Commons), 5th Series, 433 (February 10, 1947): 82.

[27]Ibid., p. 115.

[28]Ibid., p. 122.

[29]Ibid.

[30]Ibid., p. 123.

[31]Great Britain, Parliament, *Parliamentary Debates* (Commons), 5th Series, 439 (July 8, 1947): 2150.

[32]Gardner, *Sterling-Dollar Diplomacy*, p. 312.

[33]*Manchester Guardian* and *Economist* as quoted in Gardner, *Sterling-Dollar Diplomany*, pp. 314-315.

[34]Attlee Papers, M. S. 131, 1937-1947 (Bodleian Library, Oxford University).

[35]Ibid.

[36]"Exhaustion of the Dollar Credit," Memo by the Chancellor of the Exchequer, March 21, 1947, in Sir Richard Clarke (R. W. B. Clarke), *Anglo-American Collaboration in War and Peace* (Oxford: University Press, 1982), pp. 156-157.

[37]Ibid.

[38]Elisabeth Barker, *The British Between the Superpowers*, 1945-1950 (Toronto: University of Toronto Press, 1983), p. 67; see also, Victor Rothwell, *Britain and the Cold War, 1941-1947* (London: Jonathan Cope, 1982), Chapter 8, "Britain, the United States and Western Europe, 1944-1947."

[39]*Manchester Guardian*, July 25, 1947.

[40]Bullock, *Ernest Bevin, Foreign Secretary, 1945-1951*, pp. 441-443.

[41]Attlee Papers, M. S. 131, 1937-1947 (Bodleian Library, Oxford University).

[42]Ibid.

[43]Great Britain, Parliament, *Parliamentary Debates* (Commons), 5th Series, 443 (October 23, 1947): 266-268.

[44]Great Britain, Parliament, *Parliamentary Debates* (Commons), 5th Series, 441 (August 7, 1947): 1798-1799.

[45]Great Britain, Parliament, *Parliamentary Debates* (Commons), 5th Series,441 (August 8, 1947): 1801.

[46]Ibid., p. 1805.

[47]Ibid.

[48]Great Britain, Parliament, *Parliamentary Debates* (Commons), 5th Series, 441 (August 11, 1947): 1968.

[49]Great Britain, Parliament, *Parliamentary Debates* (Commons), 5th Series, 441 (August 8, 1947): 1882.

[50]Lord Chandos Papers, 4/5, Oliver Lyttelton, Letter, Oliver Lyttelton to Winston S. Churchill, August 26, 1947 (Churchill College, Cambridge).

[51]Great Britain, Parliament, *Parliamentary Debates* (Commons), 5th Series, 445 (October 28, 1947): 702.

[52]Ibid., p. 701.

[53]Ibid., p. 704.

[54]Ibid., pp. 703-704.

[55]Ibid., p. 703.

[56]Ibid., p. 707.

[57]Ibid., p. 708.

[58]Ibid.

[59]Ibid., p. 720.

[60]*News Chronicle*, August 14, 1947.

[61]Butler Papers, RAB, H, 46 "The Conservative Research Department and Conservative Recovery After 1945," Memorandum, Michael Fraser to Mr. Butler, September 6, 1961 (Trinity College, Cambridge University), p. 2.

[62]Interview, Lord Fraser of Kilmorack, London, England, House of Lords, July 24, 1986.

CHAPTER VI

CHURCHILL AND SOCIALIST BRITAIN

"The gentleman in Whitehall really does know better what is good for people, than people know themselves."

Attlees' Economic Secretary to
the Treasury, Douglas Jay, in
The Socialist Case.

The events of 1948-1949 that affected Churchill's leadership role can be separated into four categories: first, Parliamentary by-elections; next came the further organizational efforts of Lord Woolton to fund and reform the party's ability to authenticate its progressive image desired by Churchill. Paralleling these structural developments was the institutional maturing of the Conservative Research Department that emerged as the Tory "civil service." The fourth factor or category originated in the Attlee administration's attempt to finalize what Labour's 1945 election manifesto referred to as the "realization of a Socialist Commonwealth." In legislative terms, this took the form of a bill to nationalize the British iron and steel industry. Winston Churchill, whose leadership efforts had advocated government intervention in various industrial sectors, would oppose this effort to implement the creation of a "Socialist Britain."

Although a national election was not to take place until 1950, the years 1948-1949 witnessed two important Parliamentary by-elections. The first came in March 1948 in the North Croydon constituency. Robert Rhodes James has said it "was one of the most celebrated postwar by-elections."[1] Located just south of the Greater London area and composed of middle-class voters, North Croydon was held by the Conservatives in the 1945 General Election by only 607 votes.[2] When the Tory M. P., Mr. Williams, retired in February, Labour contested this seat with a strategy that was similar to that of the 1945 election. At the end of January, the Prime Minister condemned the Conservative Party as a class party which, if given power, would introduce "class" measures harmful to working class and low income groups.[3] Winston Churchill tried to diffuse this charge by responding in a London radio broadcast on February 14, 1948. He characterized postwar Socialist rule as one of bloated bureaucracy, burdensome taxation and austerity:

> A rate of war-time taxation has been maintained in a manner which has hampered and baffled enterprise and recovery in every walk of life: 700,000 more officials, all hard-working decent men and women but producing nothing themselves, have settled down upon us to administer 25,000 regulations never enforced before in time of peace.... We are in much discomfort. The austerity campaign is to have a further stimulus. There is...insufficient food for important classes of manual workers. People with small fixed incomes are very hard pressed.[4]

His message reiterated his Parliamentary strategy that argued Socialism and Socialist planners had mismanaged the economy, one now identified by its restrictions and rations. Three days before the election, he put his reputation as progressive party leader on the line by visiting North Croydon and endorsing the Tory Candidate, a local businessman, Fred Harris: "Some people say he is only a local man, a mere Croydonian, and that we ought to have a 'stunt' candidate or some 'star turn.' For my part, I recommend you stick to the people you know best and who know you best."[5]

The Conservatives not only had to overcome the Labour candidate, Harold Nicolson, the eminent journalist, but the Liberal office seeker, a famous wartime R.A.F. Commander, "Pathfinder" Bennett. What gave added importance to this election was the fact, as manager of a local Croydon food products firm, the Tory candidate had implemented the "Industrial Charter's" worker-management proposals in his firm.[6] On March 12, 1948, the results showed the Tory polled 36,200 votes, the Labourite 24,536 votes, and the Liberal 6,321 votes.[7] "The Conservatives had now increased their vote from 23,470 in 1945 to 36,200. Their majority over Mr. Nicolson and Labour, who polled 24,536, had increased to 11,644. But most of all, at North Croydon, a progressive Tory candidate who practiced and preached those industrial policies advanced by Churchill, emerged victorious."[8]

This electoral victory was soon followed by an announcement of Lord Woolton to the Conservative Central Council on March 17, 1948. The one million pound, fund-raising target had been achieved with the help of his local constituency *bloc-corp* structure.[9] Lord Woolton spoke of these funds as "good democratic money, not a political levy—and it has no qualifications or conditions attached to the acceptance of it."[10] Winston Churchill was quick to praise Lord Woolton for "this wonderful achievement."[11]

Encouraged by these electoral and financial accomplishments, Woolton undertook two other major reforms. In May 1948, a national training center was opened on lands donated by the Conservative Peer, Lord Swinton. Given the name "Swinton College" it soon developed into a Conservative educational center for the study of election strategy and party philosophy.[12]

Between July 1948 and July 1949, over 2,000 students, i.e., *bloc-corp* workers and potential office seekers, were offered 42 courses by this "staff college of the party."[13] In addition to preparing an educated cadre of party workers, Woolton knew that Churchill's attempts to create a progressive or reformist image for the Tories was hindered by the extent to which the selection of Parliamentary candidates was limited by the insistence of the constituency associations on financial contributions from such candidates. Aware that the party could not be regarded as "classless" if working men could not afford to stand as candidates, Woolton had also noticed that "the organization was weakest in those places where a wealthy candidate had made it unnecessary for the members [of the constituency association] to collect...subscriptions."[14] Instead of openly criticizing the constituency associations, he pushed for the implementation of a resolution passed at the 1947 Brighton Party Conference, which had called for a study of the possibility of limiting subscriptions which M. P.'s and Parliamentary candidates paid to their associations.[15]

An executive committee was formed to undertake the study. It established three sub-committees: one on the financial arrangement of candidates, another on employment of local agents and the third on party finances. After receiving the reports of the sub-committees, Woolton established a "Party Committee of Inquiry into the Conservative Party Organization." His protégé, Sir David Maxwell Fyfe, (later Lord Kilmuir) was the committee's chairman. It was to issue a report on party finance and the relationship of local constituency organizations to the overall party structure. R. T. McKenzie has described the work and contributions of the Committee of Inquiry in his critically acclaimed work, *British Political Parties*. It held seventeen meetings throughout England in order to gather "evidence from a great many officers, officials and members of the party at all levels."[16] Its final product, known as the "Maxwell Fyfe Report" was presented in two volumes, an Interim Report of October 1948, and a Final Report of July 1949, which Lord Woolton then implemented as the *modus operandi* of the party. Because of these reports, the Conservative Party would require that the election expenses of candidates in each constituency was the responsibility of the local constituency associations; no subscription was to be made directly or indirectly by a candidate to fund election expenses. A Tory M. P. could make an annual subscription to his/her association but the amount "shall in no case exceed 50 pounds."[17]

Maxwell Fyfe's report followed Woolton's belief that by denying the "easy" income traditionally provided by wealthy candidates, local associations would have to improve their financial machinery in order to meet election expenses. Likewise, the Conservative Party was to publish an annual financial statement so that its finances would be a public record. These changes supported the party leader's idea of an open, democratic party that could receive a regular income to fund both long and short term programs.[18] By streamlining and broadening the financial structure of the party, Woolton was able to employ a staff of twenty full-time central office employees. Party propaganda was now channelled into two hundred factory groups and "Labour Advisory Committees" in some 274 constituency groups to spread the party's program to working class voters. By December 28, 1948, Woolton augmented his reorganization efforts when he asked for and received from Churchill the approval to establish a Conservative Trust Fund to administer the party's revenues.

The Conservative Research Department was also experiencing a process of change. By January 1948, its role included the publication of a series of pamphlets with the title, "What Do You Think?" that covered such topics as housing, trade unions and bureaucracy. These articles were distributed to constituency organizations to establish an educational bridge between this Tory think-tank and local candidates and agents. The research officers also acted as important links between the various Shadow Cabinet Ministers and front bench spokesmen because the writing of Parliamentary speeches or "briefs" had become a function of the research staff.[20] Winston Churchill relied on the Research Department for competent professional information as the quality of advice he received from the research staff contributed to the effectiveness of his own activities as spokesman for the party.[21] Lord Fraser recalled that the best way to supply information to Churchill was through short and concise memoranda devoid of long sentences or emotional appeals. Basically, Churchill responded best to problem-facts-solutions reports.[22] Churchill made the Conservative Research Department staff attend the weekly meetings of the party chairman, chief whips in both Lords and Commons, and backbench leaders where tactical decisions on Parliamentary subjects were discussed and finalized. It was the technical nature of debate and legislation on economic affairs during the Opposition Years, together with the place of importance the party leaders assigned to the Research Department that led to its development into the party's civil service.[23]

In November 1948, after consulting with Butler, Churchill merged the Research Department with the Party Secretariat (whose job had also been Parliamentary speech writing) and the party's Information Department.[24] The idea was to prevent any overlapping of functions and to specify responsibilities. Butler was again appointed as the chairman of this new Research Department whose duties were: providing staff to Conservative Parliamentry committees, preparing speeches of M. P.'s, disseminating information to local candidates and agents, and studying and formulating party policy.[25] Churchill's efforts to fine-tune the Research Department in order to improve its output and efficiency was going to be needed as he faced Labour's attempts to implement its 1945 political manifesto.

Following the economic developments of 1947, the Attlee government sought to stabilize the British economy. The leading figure of this effort was the Chancellor of the Exchequer, Sir Stafford Cripps. Britain's chief economic officer was the quintessence of paradox. Trained in the law, this Socialist amassed a considerable fortune by defending large corporations accused of fraud and monopoly charges. A devout Christian and High Anglican churchman, he found in the tenets of Marxism a rational blueprint for reshaping Britain's postwar industries. Known for an ascetic style, this tall, thin, bifocaled teetotaller and vegetarian "appeared almost to enjoy the austerity and self-flagellation that he exhorted the nation to adopt."[26] His policy concentrated on reviving and expanding exports at the expense of re-equipping industrial plants. To prevent inflation from damaging the export drive, heavy war-time taxation was retained to drain off purchasing power. In addition, physical controls were employed: imports were restricted and exporter's receipts of foreign currency had to be reviewed by the state; investments of all kinds, including the building of houses, was limited and consumption of clothing and foodstuffs was rationed.[27]

Under Cripps, the British citizen was asked to make do with a weekly ration of thirteen ounces of meat, one and a half ounces of cheese, six ounces of butter and margarine, one ounce of cooking fat, two pints of milk and a solitary egg. For all his unconventional ways and harsh methods, credit should be given to Cripps' policy. British export figures in December 1948 were 25 percent above those for 1947 and the largest in volume since 1929.[28] Yet, in spite of this accomplishment, it was the large injection of Marshall Aid during 1948-1949 that greatly stimulated the British economy.[29] Even Lord President Morrison stated in May 1948 that without Marshall funding unemployment in England would have risen by over 1.5 million workers.[30]

Public ownership was at the center of the socialist vision. This was reflected in what *Let Us Face the Future* referred to as the creation of a "Socialist Commonwealth." Labour's Parliamentary efforts for nationalizing coal, gas, electricity and transport had taken 530 hours in the House of Commons and 675 hours in the Lords.[31] To finalize the vision, the Attlee government introduced legislation for the control of the iron and steel industry in the October 1948 Parliamentary session. Except for various details, the Conservatives had not opposed the nationalization legislation. But by 1948, England had already experienced a major balance of payments crisis which had been accompanied by an acute shortage of steel. Unlike the other nationalized industries, the takeover of iron and steel represented a foray into manufacturing sectors of the economy. Engineering, machine tools and new and other potentially productive areas of the metallurgical trades would be seriously affected.

Since the 1930's, the steel industry had enjoyed extensive legislative protection, the continuation of which was made conditional on reorganization. This was coordinated by the British Iron and Steel Federation, formed in 1934, by the various trade associations and given wide powers by them. During the Second World War the staff of the Federation was absorbed into the Iron and Steel Control Board which ran the industry under directions from the Ministry of Supply. At the end of the war, the Federation was asked by the Churchill Coalition Government to prepare a five year program of development, which, if found acceptable to the government and if not dependent on government aid, the iron and steel industry was to be allowed to proceed under such public supervision as was necessary.[32] The Conservatives had found little reason to criticize the Federation, which possessed an adequate record of labor relations, having instituted at the end of the war a 48-hour work week. No major strike had occurred since 1926.

Clement Attlee's top governmental officials were split over proceeding with their iron and steel bill. Hugh Dalton, who the Prime Minister had restored to Cabinet rank on June 1, 1948, as Chancellor of the Duchy of Lancaster, pushed for the enactment of the bill, while Morrison, who had even opposed listing iron and steel as a nationalized target in the 1945 manifesto, was against the measure. The Lord President felt the bill would frighten away middle-class voters who were being asked by Cripps to endure a vigorous rationing system.[33] Aneurin Bevan, a leader of the Labour Party's left wing, was vehement in his support of the bill. He focused less on the arguments of productivity and more on the place of steel nationalization as a guarantee of the government's long-term commitment to socialism. Likewise, Cripps also favored the bill. Yet, another complicating factor for Attlee was Britain's advocacy of public ownership of the steel industry in the Ruhr, that is, the British zone of occupied Germany. It was difficult to argue the case for nationalization in Germany, while denying it in Britain itself. To avoid a political fissure in his Cabinet and to satisfy past appeals for a "Socialist Commonwealth," the Labour government proceeded with its plans to nationalize the iron and steel industry. In order to insure a quick passage of the measure, the Labour Party simultaneously proposed that the Parliament Act of 1911, which had reduced the House of Lords power of delaying legislation for two years, be amended. The Attlee government asked that the Conservative-dominated upper chamber's delaying power be limited to just one year.[34]

Churchill's approach to the nationalization of iron and steel was announced on October 9, 1948, at the party's annual conference held in Llandudno, Wales.[35] He again relied on two familiar themes—one constitutional—that the attempt to alter the power of the House of Lords was an attack on the traditions of the British political system, and the other economic—that the Socialist effort to control yet another industrial sector was unjustified and unnecessary given the successful operation and complexity of the iron and steel industry. Twenty days later in the House of Commons, he spoke again on these themes. When Herbert Morrison claimed that the House of Lords was "biased" and "dominated by one political party,"[36] Churchill countered with the argument that the powers of review of the upper chamber should be respected, not reduced, as its function "is essentially one of safeguarding and delaying violent or subversive measures which may endanger the long-gathered heritage of the whole people."[37] He then asked: given Britain's dependence on Marshall Aid or "subsidies,"[38] was it economically feasible to transfer another industry, which operated at a profit, to governmental control?

On November 15, 1948, the Minister of Supply, George Strauss, presented the finalized version of the iron and steel bill for Parliamentary ratification. A new Iron and Steel Corporation was to be brought into existence that would own all the securities of the major concerns at the core of the industry, that is, those responsible for iron ore, pig iron and ingot steel.[39] The total number of firms scheduled for transfer was 107. These companies employed approximately 200,000 workers.[40] Yet, the general structure of the privately-owned steel industry, including its overall selling and trading structure would be kept intact. The bill would take over companies en bloc, not reorganize or restructure them. The proposed vesting day was set for May 1, 1950.

On November 16, 1948, Churchill once again addressed the issue of the iron and steel bill. He initially sought to defuse any ideological overtones of his argument: "This is not a case of one side seeking to nationalise an industry and the other side trying to preserve an uncontrolled, unsupervised monopoly or cartel without regard to the public interest."[41] The Conservative Party, in opposing this bill, was striving to achieve the operational excellence of the industry while supporting the necessary safeguards to limit price levels in the interest of the consumer and small producer.[42] Supplied with an analysis of the steel industry by the Conservative Research Department, the Tory leader reviewed the record of the industry: production had risen from 5 million tons in 1932 to 13 million tons in 1939; total production in 1948 was at a record level of 15.5 million tons.[43] Also:

> Steel is, of course, the main prop of our export trade. Nothing is perfect on the human stage, but one could hardly point to any other instance of an industry which plays so great a part in our productive effort...without in any degree embarking on the exploitation of the consumer or harsh or improper practices.[44]

Labour's bill sought a vertical division of the industry,[45] thus creating a monopoly or cartel. But asked Churchill: what has been the record of other nationalized industies? The coal industry witnessed a rise in prices of 20 percent whether "it be for the home firesides or for the public services, power, heat, light and transport."[46] The nationalized railways also reported heavy losses for 1948.[47] To strengthen his case that the bill would disrupt a well-run industry, he quoted a statement made on November 13, 1948, by the Secretary of the Iron and Steel Confederation, the trade union leader, Lincoln Evans, that by mandating May 1, 1950, as the vesting date this: "means inevitably that steel nationalisation is to be made a major issue at the next General Election, and the industry is therefore to become a focal point of a bitter political conflict. We would have preferred it otherwise."[48] When Churchill finished, Sir Stafford Cripps addressed the issue of the price of steel shares that the government would have to pay if the steel industry was to come under government control. It became obvious that the Chancellor of the Exchequer's price index had not been adequately prepared. This allowed Churchill to argue that the bill sacrificed the public interest to the convenience of government:

> Cripps: It is an index which is rather more inclusive and more accurate than others which are kept.
>
> Churchill: The whole point is whether the index is open to the public or whether these are some figures of which the right hon. and learned Gentleman enjoys a state monopoly?
>
> Cripps: It is not a public index.[49]

The debate in the House ended with a Labour victory. But the conflict over iron and steel was to be carried over into the new year when the House of Lords rejected the bill. The Attlee government would again submit the bill to the House, but by the time it did, yet another economic crisis threatened his party's Socialist hopes.

In February 1949, the attention of the Conservative Party shifted temporarily from the debate over the steel bill to a Parliamentary by-election in the constituency of South Hammersmith. There the Tories were counting on what looked like a promising opportunity in this borderline London seat to put the party on the road to victory at the next general election, which could not be postponed beyond the summer of 1950. South Hammersmith had recorded substantial Conservative majorities in the 1930's, but in 1945 the Labour candidate, a Mr. W. T. Adams, received 12,502 votes against 9,044 for the sitting Conservative member, Sir Douglas Cooke.[50]

Prior to the vote of February 23, 1949, the Labour Government had been startled by allegations of corruption at the Board of Trade, which had not helped its by-election prospects. But the Prime Minister skillfully moved to protect his party's image when he called for a special tribunal to investigate any alleged illegal activities. When it was discovered that a Labour official, Mr. Belcher, was tainted with the improper use of the bankruptcy laws, Attlee asked for and was given Belcher's resignation. However, Churchill did not aggressively pursue the affair. He accepted and praised Attlee's handling of the matter, and even expressed pity for the disgraced official.[51]

Churchill stumped the middle-class London borough constituency in support of the 35 year old engineer and Tory candidate, Anthony Fell. At Brackenbury Road, Churchill attacked the government for its economic policies, claiming that Labour's social reforms were not financed out of economic gains in productivity, but by American Marshall funds.[52] On the night of the twenty-third of February, 1949, the votes were counted. Anthony Fell had increased the Conservative vote to 13,600, a gain of over 4,000 from the 1945 figure, but lost by 1,613 votes. However, the Labour vote was 15,223, a rise of more than two and one-half thousand votes.[53] What had happened?

It can be said that Churchill failed to translate Labour's discomfort over the Belcher affair into an electoral victory. Still, the cause of defeat ran deeper. As early as June 20, 1948, *The Times* had called for the issuance of a Tory election manifesto that was more inclusive than the *Industrial Charter*, which was addressed to domestic issues.[54] The *Economist*, in an article following the Tory defeat in South Hammersmith, blamed the Tory leader for not presenting the local voters with such a manifesto.[55] Historically, such Tory leaders as Disraeli opposed the issuance of detailed manifestoes, claiming that to do so could render an opposition party a mere imitation of a standing government. Until the South Hammersmith set-back, Churchill had followed this practice, but Labour's victory made Churchill change his strategy. He faced this issue on March 3, 1949, at a packed meeting of the 1922 committee, that is, the Conservative backbench members of the House of Commons. He did not try to hide his disappointment over the defeat, but attempted to rally his colleagues by asking them not to "be cowed because of a bump here and there."[56] The Tories lost, but the party's vote had been increased over the 1945 figure by more than four and one-half thousand votes. He also announced that the publication of a formal election manifesto, stating a progressive Tory program, was now a priority. His next move was to establish a committee that consisted of Anthony Eden, Woolton, Macmillan, Maxwell Fyfe, and David Clarke in order to create an election manifesto.[57] The actual drafting was carried out by Clarke and Michael Fraser.[58] By July 23, 1949, the document, "The Right Road for Britain" was published. Its overall message reflected the themes of Churchill's Parliamentary arguments:

> The Labour Party is trying to create a completely Socialist Britain. The vast State monopolies which are being set up are but one aspect of a society in which all forms of power are to be centralized in the Government.... In practice Socialism is proving to be restrictive and negative.... Socialism is cumbersome and inefficient.[59]

In terms of domestic policy the *Right Road* followed the direction given by the *Industrial Charter*. Conservatives promised to increase housing starts as part of their plan to create a property-owning democracy; social services were no longer, even in theory, to be a form of poor relief as adequate levels of social security, housing and employment were to be the basis of any Conservative social welfare program.[60]

Labour's high level of taxation was blamed for discouraging savings and industrial investment, as Tory plans for reduction of direct taxation would provide the necessary stimulant and incentive to increase national production and achieve prosperity. The *Right Road* was the first official Conservative statement since 1945 to combine both domestic and foreign policy issues.[61] The *Manchester Guardian* praised the document, finding it a better prepared manifesto than Labour's program, *Labour Believes in Britain*, which was published on April 11, 1949.[62] Both the *Spectator*[63] and the *Economist*[64] were critical as they claimed the Tory manifesto was vague and uninspiring.

On the day of the *Right Road*'s publication, Churchill gave a major speech of endorsement at Wolverhampton. He spoke of the manifesto's commitment to humanize, not nationalize industry, which had been a policy of failure.[65] The Tories, if returned to power, would not revoke the legislation of the last four years, but instead, the party would implement the *Industrial Charter* formulas of job security and incentives for both workers and managers. A new Conservative government would maintain close contacts with trade union leaders in order to discuss programs that would improve working conditions in British industry. Also, Churchill stressed the importance that the party's new manifesto placed on maintaining "the value, responsibility and independence of the British trade union [which] is one of the principal aims of Conservatism and Tory Democracy."[66]

After a meeting of the Labour Cabinet in February 1949, at Shaklin, on the Isle of Wight, the party began to distance itself from the ideal of nationalization.[67] A perceptive

Manchester Guardian article of February 26, 1949, spoke of a government:

> with very grave doubts about whether the technique so far adopted has been the right one...the party's difficulty is largely psychological. It has talked nationalization for thirty years; it cannot conceive of a programme without a lot of nationalization. But it finds itself...with doubts whether the ground it has already seized is not crumbling underfoot.[68]

Indeed, it must have appeared to the Prime Minister that the ground was getting shaky. In the May 1949 elections for the London City Council, a traditional Labour electoral fief, the Conservatives emerged victorious bringing to an end this constituency's annual May Day red banner parade.[69] By July 29, 1949, England witnessed a series of dock strikes in Bristol, Liverpool and London as angry dockworkers protested the government's wage restraint policy.[70] But a far graver crisis was brewing on the domestic front.

Once again dollar reserves began to fall, $76 million in March 1949 as the price of raw materials purchased from the United States increased sharply.[71] On May 19, 1949, it was reported that the weekly rate of the dollar deficit was substantially above the projected target and the outlook was gloomy. Britain was experiencing what economists called the "problem" of hard and soft currencies. Sir Stafford Cripps' export policy was able to claim that it had greatly reduced the nation's trading deficit by the end of 1948. Despite this effort, the gains in trade had not been great enought in the "hard" dollar markets. The export policy had been successful mostly in non-dollar or "soft" trading areas. Thus, the dollar deficit had not been reduced as what had been accomplished was the generation of larger balances of "soft" currencies.

Early in 1949, there were signs of an incipient recession in the United States, which did not bode well for the United Kingdom's balance of payments. The declining American business boom led to a sharp drop in dollar earnings. As speculative pressure increased on the pound, the drain on British dollar reserves gathered speed. They fell by $39 million in the week of July 10-16, 1949. These reserves then totalled $1,564 million on July 10, 1949, but England's reserves continued to fall relentlessly to $1,487 million on July 27; to $1,439 million by August 27 and to $1,410 million on September 3, 1949.[72] If the decline continued, the British could be facing financial bankruptcy.

Clement Attlee's government had two financial options. It could introduce a policy of deflation, that is, restrict the money supply. But this had been the policy of the 1930's, and as such, was contrary to party policy. It would also jeopardize Labour's re-election chances in the general election to be held in 1950. The other policy alternative, that of devaluation of the pound appeared to be the better choice. If the dollar exchange rate of $4.03 was lowered, British goods would be cheaper in world markets, especially the American market. But Cripps seemed to reject this option when he told the House of Commons on July 6, 1948, that the government would not devalue its currency.[73]

On July 21, 1949, Cripps, suffering from insomnia from his regular 14-16 hour work days, sought recovery in a Swiss sanatorium. British economic policy was put into the hands of a rising young Labour politician, Hugh Gaitskill, then Minister of Fuel and Power, the President of the Board of Trade, Harold Wilson, and the Economic Secretary to the Treasure, Douglas Jay. Hugh Gaitskill and Jay advocated devaluation, while Jay claims Wilson "took refuge in ambiguity."[74] Clement Attlee's biographer writes that it was Gaitskill's and Jay's arguments that convinced the Prime Minister to accept devaluation.[75] The Minister of Fuel's argument was that only devaluation would make export to dollar markets more profitable, therefore making prospects of an expansion in dollar earnings more favorable. Also, there was a danger of a currency collapse if the reserves continued to fall.[76] By July 29, 1949, Attlee wrote to Cripps in Switzerland informing his Chancellor of the change in policy.[77] On August 19, 1949, Cripps returned to office and plans were made to receive American blessings for devaluating. Talks began in Washington on August 29, 1949, and despite what both George Kennan and Dean Acheson, described as a "cold reception" from the United States Secretary of the Treasury, John Snyder,[78] the Americans approved the policy, which took effect on September 18, 1949. Churchill interpreted Labour's response to this sterling crisis as the bankruptcy of Socialist economic policy. This argument was presented in four speeches: three in the House of Commons on September 28, 1949, October 24 and October 27, 1949, while the other came at the annual Conservative Conference at Empress Hall, Earls Court, London on October 14, 1949. He began on September 28th in a moderate tone: "no one must under-rate the task which fell upon these Labour Ministers as the consequence of the Election of 1945."[79]

England had a substantial adjustment of reverting to a peace-time economy. Yet, despite these acknowledged difficulties, Labour's record has not given the economy the steady, productive direction the nation needed. Instead, "they have taken 40 percent of the national income for the purpose of Government Administration. Our taxation has been the highest in the world. It oppresses every effort and transaction of daily life."[80] Devaluation was criticized not because it might increase British exports to the dollar market, but is was defective as it would raise the price of imports, inflating the economy and negatively affecting those living on fixed or slowly rising incomes.[81] At the Conservative Party Conference, London, Churchill offered the Tory alternatives:

> The *Right Road for Britain* shows where we want to go. It offers a broad, tolerant, progressive and hopeful prospect to the British people.... It constitutes an overwhelming repudiation of the taint that we are a class party seeking to defend abuses or willing to tolerate the exploitation of the mass of the people by vested interests, by monopolies or by bygone ideas.[82]

When Attlee explained the further domestic ramifications of devaluation—that its implementation would bring cuts in government spending for education and housing,[83] increased taxes[84] and reduced imports of consumer goods,[85] Churchill again spoke in terms of Socialist mismanagement by claiming such measures would not have been necessary if adequate financial planning that did not harm rich productive industries such as iron and steel had been given priority over well-meaning but dated economic concepts.[86]

Herbert Morrison attacked the above statement, claiming Churchill's rhetoric was typical of the Tory party "because they are always spitefully-minded people."[87] The Lord President then blundered by mentioning the cuts in unemployment benefits that had been made in September, 1931. Thus, Churchill and Conservative M. P. for Aberdeen, Robert Boothby, were quick to remind Morrison that it had not been a Conservative who introduced such cuts, but the Labour Chancellor of the Exchequer, Mr. Snowden, just as another Labour Chancellor, Sir Stafford Cripps, now sought to reduce housing and education subsidies, something which the Conservative *Right Road* sought to avoid.[88] Churchill concluded his criticism of government economic policy by reemphasizing Conservative domestic themes-reduced taxation, efficient planning and a lessening of governmental controls of industry.[89]

By November 1949, the Tory leader knew that he could not prevent passage of the steel bill. Yet, owing to Labour's economic difficulties, his strategy now sought to forestall, as much as was possible, the implementation of the bill before the next Parliamentary election. On November 2nd and 3rd, 1949, Churchill, together with Tory Lords Woolton, Salisbury and Swinton met to discuss how this plan could be accomplished.[90] It was decided that Conservative acquiescence both in the Commons and the Lords to the steel bill would be given on the condition that the government would: (1) delay appointing officials to the control mechanism of the bill, that is, the officers who would manage the new Steel Board; and (2) change the vesting day for the bill to the end of January 1951.[91] Winston Churchill told Lord Swinton, who was chosen to approach Minister Strauss, that if Labour accepted these amendments, the Tories would not oppose the bill. When the Attlee government accepted this plan,[92] its bill passed both Houses, receiving Royal Assent at the end of November 1949, three months before the general election of February 1950. Vesting day was set for February 1951.

The November 2nd and 3rd meetings were important for another reason. It was becoming more apparent that a general election would soon be announced. Labour wanted to face the electorate before the effects of devaluation in higher import costs worked their way through to the price of goods in the shops.[93] Clement Attlee was well aware that by the spring of 1950 both the factories and shops would be experiencing government cuts of 100 million pounds in dollar imports in food and consumer goods. There were bound to be more shortages, and even unemployment. On top of these conditions would be the restrictive effects of the curtailment in capital expenditure and administrative cuts.[94] Likewise, Churchill knew by the time of the November meeting that Butler's Conservative Research Department had distributed to the local constituency associations over 2,000 copies of the party's manifesto, the *Right Road*.[95] Also, at the November meeting, Lord Woolton told the Tory leader that "the Party machine was all geared up for an election, and from the point of view of the operation of the Party machine, the sooner the election came the better.... He thought in a January election we should get a majority of 80."[96] A majority of 80!, but was this possible?

Churchill's Parliamentary and party speeches had criticized Labour's domestic policy, not because it adopted the conception of the welfare state, but because it was based on the philosophy that the "gentlemen in Whitehall knew better," an ideal of a Socialist Britain that had resulted in a society based on inefficient planning, monetary and financial mismanagement, scarcity, rationing and a lack of adequate housing for middle- and lower-income groups. But could his opposition to "Socialist Britain" be translated into electoral victory?

As the year 1949 ended, the Conservative leader, unlike in July 1945, was supported by a party structure that no longer required Conservative Parliamentary candidates to contribute a minimum 100 pounds a year to a constituency association to gain acceptance as the party's nominee. Thanks to Lord Woolton's efforts, the Tories had also established a system of trained, paid and experienced bloc and corp agents throughout the country to channel Tory election materials and mobilize votes. An enlarged Research Department had emerged, which with Churchill's support, now insured the preparation of progressive policies, the culmination of which was the *Right Road for Britain*. Given these developments, Churchill told his colleagues at the conclusion of the November 1949 meeting that he now favored an election—the sooner the better.[97]

Notes

[1] Robert Rhodes James (ed.), *Winston S. Churchill, His Complete Speeches, 1897-1963*, Vol. VII, *1943-1949*, p. 7613.

[2] *London Times*, "Croydon Won by Conservative," March 12, 1948, p. 4f.

[3] Attlee Papers, M. S. 132, 1948-1949 (Bodleian Library, Oxford Universit).

[4] James, *Winston S. Churchill, His Complete Speeches, 1987-1963*, Vol. VII, *1943-1949*, pp. 75-93.

[5] Ibid., p. 7613.

[6] *London Times*, "Croydon 'Whale of a Setback'", March 13, 1948, p. 3a.

[7] *London Times*, "Croydon Won by Conservative," March 12, 1948, p. 4f.

[8] Ibid.

[9] Conservative Research Department Files, "CC04/2/96-104," "Lord Woolton's Fighting Fund" Targets—Announcement, March 17, 1948 (Bodleian Library, Oxford University).

[10] Ibid.

[11]Woolton papers, M. S. Woolton, 21, Correspondence as Chairman, Conservative Party, Letter, Winston S. Churchill to Lord Woolton, March 18, 1948.

[12]Conservative Research Department, "CC04/2/79-95," "Lord Woolton's Fighting Fund" 194701948(2), Swinton College, New Conservatism.

[13]*Conservative Party Conference Report*, 1948 (London), p. 18.

[14]Earl of Woolton, *Memoirs*, p. 345.

[15]*Conservative Party Conference Report*, 1947 (London), p. 28.

[16]Robert Trelford McKenzie, *British Political Parties: The Distribution of Power Within the Conservative and Labour Parties*, 2nd ed. (New York: Praeger, 1964), p. 183.

[17]Interim and Final Reports of the Committee on Party Organization, 1948 and 1949 (London), p. 26.

[18]Hoffman, *The Conservative Party in Opposition, 1945-1951*, p. 120.

[19]Woolton Papers, M. S. Woolton, 21, Correspondence as Chairman, Conservative Party, Letter, Lord Woolton to Winston S. Churchill, December 28, 1948.

[20]Anthony Barker and Michael Rush, *The Member of Parliament and His Information* (London: Allen and Unwin, 1970), p. 250.

[21]David Clarke, "The Organization of Political Parties," *Political Quarterly* 21 (1950): 88.

[22]Interview, Lord Fraser of Kilmorack, London, England, House of Lords, July 24, 1986.

[23]Ronald Butt, "Tory Civil Service," *Times* (London), (20 December 1969), p. 1.

[24]Butler Papers, RAB, H. 46, "The Conservative Research Department and Conservative Recovery after 1945," Memorandum, Michael Fraser to Mr. Butler, September 6, 1961 (Trinity College, Cambridge University), p. 5.

[25]Ibid., p. 7.

[26]Morgan, *Labour in Power, 1945-1951*, p. 363.

[27]R. S. Milne, "Britain's Economic Planning Machinery," *American Political Science Review* 46 (1952): 406.

[28]Morgan, *Labour in Power, 1945-1951*, p. 368.

[29]Great Britain, Parliament, *Parliamentary Debates* (Commons), 5th Series, 457 (October 28, 1948): 536.

[30]Great Britain, Parliament, *Parliamentary Debates* (Commons), 5th Series, 458 (November 16, 1948): 217.

[31]Sir Norman Chester, *The Nationalization of British Industry, 1945-1951*, pp. 1004-1006.

[32]Ibid., p. 159.

[33]Attlee Papers, M. S. 132, 1948-1949 (Bodleian Library, Oxford University).

[34]Great Britain, Parliament, *Parliamentary Debates* (Commons), 5th Series, 458 (November 17, 1948): 484.

[35]James, *Winston S. Churchill, His Complete Speeches, 1897-1963*, Vol. VII, *1943-1949*, p. 7715.

[36]Great Britain, Parliament, *Parliamentary Debates* (Commons), 5th Series, 457 (October 28, 1948): 273.

[37]Ibid., p. 261.

[38]Ibid., p. 263.

[39]Great Britain, Parliament, *Parliamentary Debates* (Commons), 5th Series, 458 (November 15, 1948):59.

[40]Ibid., p. 71.

[41]Great Britain, Parliament, *Parliamentary Debates* (Commons), 5th Series, 458 (November 16, 1948): 218.

[42]Ibid.

[43]Ibid.

[44]Ibid., p. 219.

[45]Ibid., p. 223.

[46]Ibid., p. 227.

[47]Great Britain, Parliament, *Parliamentary Debates* (Commons), 5th Series, 458 (November 16, 1948): 228.

[48]Ibid., p. 232.

[49]Ibid., p. 314.

[50]Goodhart with Branston, *The 1922, The Story of the Conservative Backbenchers Parliamentary Committee*, p. 144.

[51]Great Britain, Parliament, *Parliamentary Debates* (Commons), 5th Series, 460 (February 3, 1949): 1836.

[52]James, *Winston S. Churchill, His Complete Speeches, 1987-1963*, Vol. VII, *1943-1949*, p. 7741.

[53]Goodhart with Branston, *The 1922, The Story of...Committee*, p. 149.

[54]*Sunday Times*, "Can the Conservative Win?", June 20, 1948.

[55]*The Economist* as quoted in Goodhart with Branston, *The 1922, The Story of...Committee*, pp. 144-146.

[56]Ibid., p. 147.

[57]Butler Papers, RAB, H, 46 "The Conservative Research Department and Conservative Recovery After 1945," Memorandum, Michael Fraser to Mr. Butler, September 6, 1961 (Trinity College, Cambridge University), p. 5.

[58]Ibid.

[59]*The Right Road for Britain*, in the *New Conservatism* (London: Conservative Political Center, 1955), p. 48.

[60]Ibid., p. 41.

[61]Butler Papers, RAB, H, 46, "The Conservative Research Department and Conservative Recovery After 1945," Memorandum, Michael Fraser to Mr. Butler, September 6, 1961 (Trinity College, Cambridge University), p. 5.

[62]*Manchester Guardian*, "Tory Socialism?" July 23, 1949.

[63]*Spectator*, "Right Road?" July 24, 1949.

[64]*Economist*, "The Tory Alternative," July 30, 1949.

[65]James, *Winston S. Churchill, His Complete Speeches, 1897-1963*, Vol. VII, *1943-1949*, p. 7832.

[66]Ibid.

[67]Attlee Papers, M. S. 132, 1948-1949 (Bodleian Library, Oxford University).

[68]*Manchester Guardian*, "Shanklin," Feburary 26, 1949.

[69]Attlee Papers, M. S. 132, 1948-1949 (Bodleian Library, Oxford University).

[70]Ibid.

[71]Morgan, *Labour in Power, 1945-1951*, p. 380.

[72]Ibid.

[73]Great Britain, Parliament, *Parliamentary Debates* (Commons), 5th Series, 466 (July 6, 1949): 2160.

[74]D. P. T. Jay, *Change and Fortune* (London: Hutchinson, 1980), p. 197.

[75]Harris, *Attlee*, p. 436.

[76]Philip M. Williams, ed., *The Dairy of Hugh Gaitskill 1945-1956* (London: Jonathan Cope, 1983), p. 130.

[77]Jay, *Change and Fortune*, p. 188.

[78]George F. Kennan, *Memoirs, 1925-1950* (Boston: Little, Brown and Company, 1967), p. 458; and Dean Acheson, *Present at the Creation, My Years in the State Department* (New York: W. W. Norton, Inc., 1969), p. 322.

[79]Great Britain, Parliament, *Parliamentary Debates* (Commons), 5th Series, 468 (September 28, 1949): 158.

[80]Ibid.

[81]Ibid., p. 611.

[82]James, *Winston S. Churchill, His Complete Speeches, 1897-1963*, Vol. VIII, *1943-1949*, p. 7863.

[83]Great Britain, Parliament, *Parliamentary Debates* (Commons), 5th Series, 468 (October 24, 1949): 1017.

[84]Ibid., p. 1018.

[85]Ibid., p. 1021.

[86]Ibid., p. 1024.

[87]Great Britain, Parliament, *Parliamentary Debates* (Commons), 5th Series, 468 (October 27, 1949): 1550.

[88]Ibid., pp. 1549-1552: 1616-1617.

[89]Ibid., p. 1623; see also R. A. Butler, "Conservative Policy," *Political Quarterly* 20 (1949).

[90]Swinton Papers (Philip Cunliffe-Lister), Memorandum, "Secret," "Iron and Steel," November 15, 1949. Meeting with Winston S. Churchill, p. 1.

[91]Ibid., pp. 1-2.

[92]Ibid., p. 3

[93]Attlee Papers, M.S. 132, 1948-1949 (Bodleian Library, Oxford University).

[94]Ibid.

[95]Butler Papers, RAB, G, 20, 1-52, September 1949, *The Right Road for Britain*, "Tory Constituencies," (Trinity College, Cambridge, England).

[96]Swinton papers (Phillip Cunliffe-Lister), Memorandum, "Secret," "Iron and Steel," November 15, 1949, Meeting with Winston S. Churchill, p. 2.

[97]Ibid.

CHAPTER VII

RECOVERY AND VICTORY

"Politics is at least a struggle for power."

Samuel Beer, *Modern
British Politics.*

In the twenty-two month period between January 1950
and October 1951, the British political system experienced
two general elections. The Conservatives fought both
campaigns under the banner of "anti-socialism," but this
term should not be confused with the crude laissez faire
slogan of their 1945 election effort. Instead, the Tories
presented to the voter a much more sophisticated appeal,
one that included not only the acceptance of the welfare
state, but the effective criticism of the government's policies
of rationing, planning and austerity. By associating his party
with this theme, Churchill would attempt to replace the
government of Clement Attlee. Unlike the 1945 election,
foreign policy would not be used by Churchill in 1950 to
differentiate his party from that of Attlee's. Until Churchill's
private papers are open to review one can only speculate as
to this choice of strategy. One reason could be the disastrous
results reaped by the Tories from this issue in the 1945
General Election. Yet another factor could be the broad
agreement over the direction of postwar British foreign
relations that evolved from the close wartime relationship
between Churchill and Labour's Foreign Secretary, Ernest

Bevin. As Sir Frank Roberts, Bevin's principal Private Secretary wrote:

> When I accompanied Bevin to international meetings after the war...he never missed an opportunity to speak warmly of Churchill and to draw attention to this close wartime relationship.... And from this sprang the close postwar understanding...which resulted on major matters in what amounted to a bi-partisan foreign policy.[1]

Given Robert's comment, it is interesting to note the conclusion of H. G. Nicholas in his study of the 1950 General Election as to why foreign affairs did not play a significant role in this contest: "Foreign affairs does not easily lend itself to electoral debate, least of all when there is substantial agreement between the major parties."[2]

On January 10, 1950, the Prime Minister, without consulting his chief election strategist, Morrison, announced the dissolution of Parliament with polling day to take place on February 23rd. Churchill, who had been vacationing in Madeira, returned immediately to England and asked Butler to meet with him at his Westerham residence on January 12, 1950, to prepare for the election.[3] He wanted Butler and the Conservative Research Department to draft an election statement that would synthesize, in broad terms, his opposition to Labour's philosophy of government.[4] A formidable undertaking was about to begin. The government had a majority in the House of Commons of 146. The Conservatives knew that to overcome so great a superiority in a single election and to obtain a working majority would be "difficult and almost unprecedented."[5] Furthermore, despite the rapport that Lord Woolton had developed with the Liberal constituency groups, the Liberal Party decided to contest the election and put up 475 candidates.

On January 18, 1950, the Labour Party issued its manifesto, *Let Us Win Through Together*, but British press reaction was critical more of what was left out than what was put in the document: "There are only passing references to the dollar crisis and the devaluation of the pound; there is no mention of Marshall aid or even of the United States or of the economies in public expenditure which were to put the economy into balance after devaluation."[6] The manifesto reflected Labour's strategy of de-emphasizing nationalization while stressing the party's contributions to full employment.[7] Herbert Morrison made sure that major controversial protagonists of nationalization, such as Aneurin Bevan, were not displayed on the national scene.[8] The appeal of Labour was to "past troubles,"[9] that is, their conscious effort was to, once again, equate the Tories with unemployment.

The Conservative manifesto, *This is the Road*, was published on January 25, 1950. It was a condensed version of *The Right Road for Britain*. Drafted by the Conservative Research Department,[10] it followed Churchill's wishes as it contained those anti-socialist themes that the Tory leader was to develop during the campaign: socialist mismanagement of the economy,[11] the low rate of housing starts,[12] the heavy burden of taxation, bureaucratic waste,[13] and respect for the role of trade unions.[14] To offset Labour's tactic of branding the Conservatives as the party of the unemployed, *This is the Road* argued that Churchill's Conservative-dominated wartime Coalition Government had initially addressed this problem in Lord Woolton's 1944 White Paper on Employment: "We made far-reaching plans, based upon hard experience and new knowledge, to cope with the evil."[15]

The Tories then quoted Morrison's admission of May 1948 that without America's Marshall Aid, unemployment under Labour's postwar government would have been well over the one million figure: "These are strange confessions...to make at a time when they are boasting that they have cured unemployment."[16] Conservative programs would not lead to jobless workers, as "We regard the maintenance of full employment as the first aim of a Conservative Government."[17] Churchill and his party would contest the election of 1950 with the message that Tory policies for employment and social services were progressive and humane, as a new Conservative administration wanted to hasten, not retard, the technical and managerial transformation of British industry.

The distribution of Parliamentary seats in 1945 had favored Labour owing to the movements of population since the constituency boundaries were last drawn in 1918. The 1950 election took place under a new legal framework because of the passage of the Representation of the People Act of 1949. This law eliminated two archaic forms of plural voting: the business premises vote, a historical survivor from the years 1832 to 1918, when the main qualification for the vote was ownership of property, and the university graduates vote. The effect of this change was minimal as only 65,000 votes were affected.

The major development, however, came with the law's revising of constituency boundaries. In 1950, the average constituency returning a Labour M. P. was to number 51,000 electors, whereas the average constituency electing a Conservative member had 57,000 electors.[18] The total number of Parliamentary seats under the new act was 625, compared to 640 in 1945. The total electorate on the October 1949 Register (on which the 1950 election was fought) numbered 34,269,764 in contrast to 32,836,419 in 1945. The reallocation of seats in terms of population reduced the importance of the non-urban areas[19] as 171 cities with a population of over 60,000 now controlled 54.6 percent of all Parliamentary sets and contained 56.5 percent of the electorate.[20] Without the urban vote, neither Labour nor Tory could obtain electoral victory. It was in competing for these votes that Lord Woolton's organizational efforts would prove their worth. Whereas the Labour Party had agents in only 279 constituencies in England, Wales and Scotland, the Tories fought the 1950 election with 527 full-time agents.[21] Most of their efforts concentrated on door-to-door canvassing to line up supporters, a good deal of loudspeaker, street-to-street talking by candidates, heavy literature distribution in the cities and an election day round-up of Conservative voters to be "sure" that an agent's constituency block was thoroughly solicited. H. G. Nicholas's study of the election concluded that the Conservatives owed at least ten new Parliamentary seats to this kind of organizational effort.[22]

The campaign itself was waged primarily on domestic issues.[23] The Gallup poll taken in January and February showed that housing, high prices of consumer goods, full employment and tax reduction were considered most important.[24] Building houses ranked the highest among voter issues at 31 percent, inflated prices 21 percent, preventing unemployment 20 percent, and reduced taxes 16 percent.[25] Unlike his 1945 election activities, Churchill closely paralleled these voter concerns. It began on January 21, 1950, with a London speech. Its message, devoid of any "Gestapo" references established his election themes:

> Socialism is based on the idea of an all-powerful State which owns everything, which plans everything, which distributes everything and thus through its politicians and officials decides the daily life of the individual citizen. We have not of course got this—or anything like it—in Britain at the present time. The process of establishing the Socialist State has only begun.
>
> The practical question which we have to settle now is whether we shall take another deep plunge into State ownership and State control, or whether we shall restore a greater measure of freedom of choice and action to our people; and of productive fertility and variety to our industry. Before deciding upon this, it is well to look around.[26]

To look around spoke of "the heaviest taxation....We are now paying 500,000 pounds more a year even than in the height of the war."[27] He found a weakened currency, where "the buying power of every pound we earn in wages, salaries or in trading...has fallen since the war stopped no less than 3s 8d. This has struck a heavy blow at the social services, at pensions of every kind."[28] Although Labour and Tory differed on the government's economic record, "on the question of unemployment there is no real difference between the two political parties....The Conservatives...regard the prevention of mass unemployment as the most solemn duty of government."[29] And on the issue of housing, the Tory leader spoke of Labour's 1945 election promise of millions of new homes, but the list of those waiting for new houses "are longer than ever...and every house costs three times as much. Surely something must have gone wrong—and very wrong."[30]

Nine days later, on January 28, 1950, in his Woodford constituency, Churchill spoke of the difficulties of postwar problems:

> When Mr. Attlee's Government came into power nearly five years ago we did not underrate the difficulties with which they would have to contend. These difficulties would have strained to the utmost all the resources of a National Government and a united nation. We did not grudge the new Ministers their offices, nor envy them their responsibilities.[31]

The Conservative Party had backed the government attempt to secure the American loan, "We hoped this would tide us over the transition from war to peace and help us to re-equip our industries."[32] But Socialist hopes of nationalization failed to modernize British industry and failed to utilize "good administration"[33] in managing the country's resources. The government then had to revert to controls and taxation to implement its Socialist vision. Taking aim at Labour's manifesto, he asked:

> Is it not surprising that in their official manifesto they should not even mention the aid they have received from the United States? There is not one word from the beginning to the end of this document, either of thanks to a generous and friendly nation, for the help on which they have lived politically or of recognition that, but for the American subsidies, mass unemployment would have fallen upon us, with all its sorrow and suffering.[34]

His concluding remarks dealt with Conservative policy toward nationalization. A Tory government would not repeal existing legislation but neither would it extend this practice to any other industries. However, there would be one exception, as the iron and steel law was to be repealed.

At Cardiff, Wales, on February 8, 1950, Churchill reminded his audience that the party he now led belonged to the "great traditions and principles of Tory democracy enunciated by Benjamin Disraeli and after him by my father, Lord Randolph Churchill".[35] It was the tradition of concern for social justice and reform that he applied when criticizing the results of Labour's housing program:

> The Socialist housing policy has turned out even worse than we feared. Under the much abused Tory rule before the war, we were able to build 1,000 permanent houses a day on this island.... In the last 4 1/2 years of the Socialist new world...we have built barely 400 permanent houses a day. The Minister of Health [Aneurin Bevan] declared: "I confidently expect that before the next election every family in Great Britain will have a separate house." In this city of Cardiff alone there are no fewer than 15,000 families on the waiting list for houses.[36]

He spoke to this urban audience of the Conservative housing policy, one that would use both the private building societies or companies and the local authorities. Labour's licensing system, which restricted the number of building starts available to the private sector, would be abolished.

Clement Attlee, like Churchill, gave only one national broadcast in this election, that of Saturday, February 18th. It "was a sober, dignified"[37] talk that described his party's success in creating the welfare state. Its major thrust was a warning to the voter that a Tory victory would bring back the "bad old days," that the Conservatives would give cake to the few and crumbs to the many. H. G. Nicholas's study found that "the most ardent supporter of its sentiments would be hard put to find...in its delivery much that was absorbing or inspiring."[38] After finishing the speech, the Prime Minister returned to his campaign activity of motoring throughout the shires with his wife at the steering wheel. Churchill, attacking "his opponents with gusto,"[39] likewise continued to campaign vigorously. During the last twelve days before polling day, concern for housing, unemployment, the cost of living and taxes were terms that he repeatedly identified with the Conservative Party. At the Davenport constituency (Plymouth), on February 9, 1950:

> Here in Plymouth I am told you have a waiting list of 11,000 houses...there are in Davenport houses which were built by private enterprise before the war in 1938 for which people paid 685 pounds. These houses sell for 2,000 pounds today. What a sign of Socialist efficiency. What a sign of getting value for money. What a sign in the fall of the purchasing power of money.[40]

At Usher Hall, Edinburgh, on February 14, 1950: "Hundreds of thousands of families are living in distressing conditions of overcrowding and discomfort made all the worse because high hopes to which they were led by the Socialist Government no longer sustain them."[41] In his single broadcast of the election series, on February 17, 1950:

> Our opponents are also telling...pensioners, as they go from door to door: The Tories will cut your pensions! But it is they who have already cut them by 3s. 9d. in the pound through the rise in prices, and the full results of devaluation.... The oppressive burden of taxation is the first problem to which a Conservative Government will turn its attention.[42]

The only exception to stressing domestic issues came in Churchill's speech in Edinburgh on February 14th. Injecting a new issue into the election campaign, the Conservative leader sought to capitalize on his elder stateman'a image, by calling for talks with Soviet Russia.[43] Bevin characterized this statement as a 'stunt,' while Morrison referred to it as 'soap-box-diplomacy.' Although the speech 'attracted world-wide attention,'[44] it did not generate widespread voter interest. Studies of the 1950 General Election have also concluded that the Edinburg speech, as well as the issue of foreign policy, did not influence the outcome of the election.[45]

On February 17, 1950, the *News Chronicle* published a Gallup poll which showed voter preferences as: Labour 45 percent, Conservatives 42.5 percent, Liberals 12 percent and others one-half percent.[46] Its last poll on February 22, 1950, carried the headline, "Election. Neck and Neck" and claimed that Labour and Tory were now so evenly matched that it declined to pick the winner.[47] An unprecedented 83.9 percent of the electorate cast a total of 28,772,671 votes. The election ended in virtually a tie. Labour returned with 315 seats and 13,331,682 votes, thus increasing its vote over 1945 by 1-1/4 million. Churchill's Conservative Party won 90 more seats than in 1945, returning to the new Parliament with 296 seats. This represented an increase of 2.5 million votes over that of 1945. The Liberals took 9 seats with 2,679,712 votes. Labour's losses were heaviest in the suburban areas of the big towns. These were the residential areas of the middle-and-lower-middle-class—the office worker and professionals. It was here that Churchill's appeals cut deeply into Labour's 1945 gains. A post election analysis of the *News Chronicle* showed: "Whereas in 1945 54% of those rated as middle class would vote Conservative, 21% Labour and 11% Liberal, by 1950 the figures had moved to 63% Conservative, 16% Labour, 13% Liberal."[48] This shift also reflected the dissatisfaction of the middle-class with the government's austerity policies.[49] Likewise, the Tories increased the percentage of their national vote that was urban, from 45 percent in 1945 to 55 percent in 1950.[50] It was the cities that produced 54.9 percent of the Conservative vote as opposed to 44.9 percent in 1945.[51]

The Conservatives also attracted a younger voter as 36 percent of those between the ages of 21 to 29 voted Tory in 1950 as opposed to only 26.5 percent in 1945; 45 percent of this age group voted Labour in 1950 in contrast with a 58 percent figure in 1945.[52] Another interesting finding of the election was the effect of Aneurin Bevan's "vermin" speech. It will be recalled that on July 7, 1948, at Belle Vue, Manchester, Bevan, the Minister of Health, had electrified the political atmosphere by denouncing the Tories as "lower than vermin."[53] Herbert Morrison in his *Memoirs* (published

1960) wrote that the remark had cost Labour two million votes in the 1950 election.[54] However, Nicholas's study of the election found that only 12 percent of the Tory candidates' addresses mentioned this speech.[55] Robert Blake in his 1985 edition of the *Conservative Party from Peel to Thatcher*, questioned the accuracy of Morrison's two million vote figure.[56] Donoughue and Jones in their 1973 publication of *Herbert Morrison: Portrait of a Politician* do not even mention Bevan's vermin speech as a factor in the election. Winston Chuchill mentioned the remark only once in a January 28, 1950, speech to his Woodford constituents.[57] Even so, Bevan's "vermin" speech became equated with Churchill's "Gestapo" speech in the minds of many voters as examples of extreme political demagoguery.

Although Labour remained in office, the election results of 1950 were quite remarkable. Labour had emerged triumphant in 1945, sweeping the country and confident of retaining power for a generation. The Tories were "a beaten army and almost a rabble."[58] Now, with its popularity reduced, Mr. Attlee's government would cling precariously to office with an overall majority in the House of Commons of six.

The 1950 Parliament conducted its business with the awareness that yet another general election might be immiment. A heavy legislative program was not attempted because a government majority could not be insured on those Standing Committees of the House which reviewed and altered potential statutes. All major bills now had to be discussed in the Committees of the Whole House where the rejuvenated Tory party could maneuver its increased numbers to bring down the government on a vote of confidence. Therefore, Labour adopted a temporizing approach towards its legislative program and appeared content to carry through the financial and other routine bills necessary for the running of the country. On important decision, the government was able to scrape by with a narrow margin as the Liberals in the Commons "almost always voted for the Government; or, on those issues on which it was impossible for them to do so, gave the Government Whips sufficient notice of their intention to avoid any danger or mishap."[59]

The new Conservative M. P.'s were said to be of an exceptionally high quality.[60] They included a future Prime Minister from Bexley, Edward Heath, along with Ian Macleod, future Conservative Minister of Health in 1951; Reginald Mauding, Chancellor of the Exchequer in the 1960's; and Christopher Soames, Historian and Master of St. Anthony's College, Oxford. Of the ninety-three new Tory members, twenty-four later became Privy Councellors and no less than forty-one became ministers.[61] Churchill, who relished a Parliamentary duel,[62] appealed to his new colleagues by pressing the government with the tactic of putting down a number of "prayers" (motions to annual ministerial orders) which forced Labour to keep its reduced forces in Parliament in many all night sessions. The House of Commons then experienced "the spectacle of aged Labour members muffled up in rugs or being pushed through the division lobbies in bathchairs,"[63] so that the government's slim majority could be maintained. Those who worked with Churchill at this time found him, "a great 'soaker' of new notions, which he would digest and brood over...before reaching a decision. Out of his own fertile, questioning mind, ideas were forever tumbling in a glorious uninhibited stream which never failed to astound those who worked with him. To work with Winston Churchill meant perpetually living on the top of one's form."[64] His first speech of the new session reflected the Tories new vitality: "I must frankly confess, as I look around, that I like the appearance of these Benches better than what we had to look at during the last 4-1/2 years. It is certainly refreshing...for me to say...we are equals."[65] In his next two speeches (March 7 and April 24) he modified his debating theme. Felix Gilbert in *The End of the European Era* described the time of Labour's rule as "constraining rather than liberating, gloomy rather than exhilarating."[66] Churchill now emphasized a constraining theme as the Tory leader differentiated Conservative philosophy from that of its Labourite opponent:

> The floor which separates the two sides of the House, so evenly balanced now, is not a gulf or class; nor does it mark a breach in fundamental brotherhood. It is one of theme and doctrine.
> …There is planning on both sides, but the aim and emphasis are different. We plan for choices, they plan for rules.[67]

This is not to suggest that the arguments of administrative mismanagement, or the endorsement of the welfare state were absent: "We are all agreed that we are not going to make our great reforms and advances at the expense of the poorest of the poor;"[68] likewise, "the customer—not the gentlemen in Whitehall—and the consumer know best."[69] Still, the Conservative leader now sought to identify his party more with the idea of less restraint and less government.

After coming so close to victory, Lord Woolton renewed his efforts to establish a working relationship with the Liberal Party, which had polled over two million votes.[70] Given their declining Parliamentary numbers, there would be far fewer Liberal candidates at the next general election, and so the second preference of Liberal voters would have an important, possibly crucial, effect on the outcome of any future Parliamentary campaign. In May 1950, Woolton asked the Tory leader to appeal publicly to the Liberals: "There will be a considerable number of life-long Liberals who will be attracted by what they regard as the broad Liberalism of the Conservative Party."[71]

Lord Woolton believed that the progressive programs that Churchill had endorsed since the Conservative defeat in 1945 would appeal to those Liberals, whose politics accepted the welfare state: "They will strengthen us not only for the next Election, but in their councils for the future."[72] Winston Churchill was not opposed to Woolton's suggestion. At Usher Hall, Edinburgh, on May 18, 1950, he spoke of the

Tory program of progressive domestic reforms set forth in *This is the Road*. Asked Churchill, does not a Liberal find this document more agreeable than the "obsolete fallacy of Socialism?"[73] He then requested Butler and the Conservative Research Department to prepare an "Overlap Prospectus" which would show where Conservative Party and Liberal Party ideas coincided. The study, given to Churchill in June 1950 concluded that the Liberal "price" for future cooperation would be the adoption by the Tories of a pledge to introduce a system of proportional representation for future Parliament elections.[74] When Conservative M. P.'s rejected these terms, Churchill followed their lead.[75] Despite Woolton's goodwill, all attempts to draw closer to the Liberal Party before the next election failed to materialize.

Although the government had few new programs to offer the nation, it did manage to enact one piece of unfinished business from its earlier programs—final control over the British iron and steel industry. Clement Attlee accomplished this takeover by changing the vesting date of the legislation.[76] Churchill's criticism of this provision contained his previous arguments, that nationalization, now referred to as "centralization of responsibility,"[77] would limit the industry's proven record of expanding production, "The Governement is, in fact, picking out for fundamental disturbance the one great basic industry which of all other deserves the prize for its efficiency and its smooth working expansion."[78] But he then tried a different tactic. On September 8, 1950, the Trades Union Congress, England's most powerful worker's organization voted to opposed the government's wage restraint policy, despite Attlee's personal appearance and plea for support before the T.U.C.[79] At this meeting, Lincoln Evans, the General Secretary of the Iron and Steel Trades Confederation, issued a report that asked the Labour Government to rethink its nationalization plans for steel.[80] Evans wanted an impartial, public board, composed of both worker and management representatives, instead of the proposed government body, the Steel

Corporation. This impartial board could attempt to reach an agreement on the future of the British steel industry. Churchill used Evan's statement to oppose Labour's legislative effort to hasten the implementation of their control over steel. He endorsed the suggestion of the leader of the iron and steel workers: "We believe that the trade unions in their report...have offered a solution which, from every angle, offers superior advantage both to the employee and to the safety and progress of our country."[81] Although the government measure to vest control under the Steel Corporation Board passed on September 9, 1950, it did so by a margin of six votes, 306 to 300.

Postwar Conservatives had argued that their party had emerged from its defeat in 1945 with a new outlook towards the problems of government and the economy, one based upon realism, upon practical requirements. Labour was said to offer only a doctrinaire approach whereas the Tories were prepared to regard each problem as it arose, be it in the social or the industrial sphere—on its own merits. This attempt by Labour to control the iron and steel industry gave Churchill the opportunity to reinforce his party's claim that Conservative policy was determined not by the demands of doctrine or the interests of any single class, but by the most effective method available, whether, as in the case of steel, the best method originated from the steel industry or from the Iron and Steel Trades Confederation.

An important by-product of the policy of austerity was decreased funding for housing. Britain's total supply of houses in 1939 was 12.5 million, of which over a third had been damaged and some 700,000 had been destroyed or rendered unlivable by the war's end. In 1945, the new government looked forward to building 750,000 new homes.

Its housing program, as administered by Aneurin Bevan, operated largely through grants to local government authorities, which had built some 55,000 homes in 1946 and 140,000 in 1947. In 1948, the financial crisis led to large cuts in housing funds and by March 1950, Bevan's plans called for the construction of 200,000 units.[82] A post-election survey of July 27, 1950, produced by the Conservative Research Department showed that every Tory candidate for Parliament had made housing a major priority in their election addresses.[83] The study also raised the question: should the party endorse a target figure as an election pledge?[84] This issue underwent a dramatic change in October 1950 when at the Annual Conservative Conference at Blackpool, delegates asked for a definite promise to build 300,000 houses a year. Butler in his *Memoirs* has described the scene in the floor of the conference hall, where calls for "300,000 Houses!" became a slogan, then a demand, finally a pledge. Lord Woolton "stepped forward to the front of the platform to declare.... This is magnificent."[85] Winston Churchill was quick to agree to the demand, stating in his conference speech on October 14, 1950, "the Tory Party puts homes for the people in the very forefront of all schemes of our development."[86] After the conference, he put the Conservative Research Department to work on a detailed analysis of just what the building of 300,000 houses a year would entail,[87] as he wanted to challenge Labour on this issue with competent evidence. The Research Department files are full of figures on standards of softwood, tons of cement, coal and bricks, figures which appeared in Churchill's housing speech to the Commons of November 6, 1950. He left no doubt about the source of his facts: " We have also made, in our own research department a considerable examination."[88] His address itemized how the Tory target of 300,000 homes would be realized: eight billion bricks were produced before the war, but only six billion were currently being produced. Of the six billion, three billion have been applied to build 160,000 houses.[89] Thus, to "build another 100,000 houses would need about two billion more bricks. That is well within the range of the pre-war brick fields. If these had not been restricted and jogged about by changes of policy, there would be plenty of bricks."[90] A further review of the cement and timber requirements followed, and then he concluded with the idea that less rules and restrictions would be needed to overcome Britain's housing shortage: "Our belief is that the fewer the controls the better; that the more freedom and enterprise can play their part the more chance there is of a fertile, prosperous and progressive community."[91]

Aneurin Bevan then argued that this rhetoric of "fewer controls" was simply old fashioned Toryism, with its laissez-faire economics which would build "for sale to the well-to-do, by speculative builders and...few houses would be built to let for the ordinary man."[92] Churchill countered by arguing a Conservative housing program would not eliminate funding for local authorities just as laws would be enforced "to prevent the diversion to any kind of luxury building, whether public or private."[93] Housing must be made England's domestic priority: "Let us have less chatter and planning and scheming for future Utopias. Let us get on with the imperative job of housing the millions who ask so little and get so little for all their efforts."[94]

Labour's failure to achieve its housing pledge had allowed Churchill to reemphasize Conservative doubts about the government's ability to manage the modern welfare state. However, yet another event, the Korean War, predicted neither by Attlee or Churchill, would raise further questions about the government's leadership. Britain's military contribution to the United Nations effort in Korea received bipartisan support. Churchill welcomed what he perceived as an opportunity to strengthen the Anglo-American relationship through British military aid to the American-led U.N. forces. Yet, the outbreak of the Korean War and its ramifications on European defense needs produced an abrupt change in the British government's priorities. This was reflected in its *Economic Survey for 1951* that announced the "first objective" of government economic policy would not be housing, but the "execution of a greatly enlarged and accelerated rearmament programme."[95]

The immediate effect in Britain from the Korean conflict was a sharp rise in the cost of imports as the rush on the world market to buy raw materials used by arms manufacturers not only drove up prices but created physical shortages that threatened to hold up production. This had a negative effect on England's balance of payments position. There were shortages of non-ferrous metals along with a falling off of coal production which caused concern over Britain's ability to produce adequate levels of coal (i.e., energy supplies). The proportion of national income annually spent on defense was seven percent before Korea. In August 1950, the Cabinet agreed to raise it to ten percent with a three year arms program that involved a total expenditure of 3,600 million pounds.[96]

Rearmament also involved the partial restoration of a war economy. Controls were renewed or extended in many different directions: over raw materials, investment, consumption, prices and employment. It limited plans for industrial plant modernization and stunted the momentum of the British export drive.[97] The arms policy was not to be carried out by Cripps, but by a new Chancellor of the Exchequer. On October 20, 1950, Cripps, who had long been ailing, resigned and was succeeded by Hugh Gaitskill. This choice was strongly criticized by Aneurin Bevan; his biographer claims the powerful leftwinger objected to the appointment of this middle-class intellectual, who had little standing with Labour's rank and file.[98]

By January 1951, the government was again presented with another coal crisis. *The Times* of January 3, 1951, described the situation:

> The autumn output drive from which much was hoped has not succeeded; output a man-shift has been little higher than it was last year at the same time and total output has been significantly less. Recruitment of miners has been disappointing...as winter withdrawals (of coal stocks) go on there will be serious local scarcities which will hit the power stations most severely.[99]

Clement Attlee then appealed to the nationalized coal industry for more output, even contemplating sending 688,000 personal letters to each of Britain's coal miners to increase production.[100] On January 11, 1951, in a national address, Attlee asked the miners to produce 3,000,000 tons of extra coal between January and April.[101] But this appeal received a serious rebuff when the leaders of Scotland's 80,000 miners rejected the Prime Minister's appeal.[102] By January 13, 1951, the Minister of Fuel and Power announced cutbacks in the delivery of coal to homes until February 28, 1951 in London, the Eastern, Southeastern, Southern and Southwest regions of England.[103]

The Prime Minister's plan for increased defense spending was announced in Parliament in January 29, 1951. Labour intended to finance its arms policy "at the expense primarily of home consumption."[104] Social programs were to be curtailed, and consumer goods would not receive priority status over arms.[105] Although Churchill and the Conservatives supported the necessity of rearmament, the Tory leader pursued his probing of what he saw as the weak points of Labour's economic methods utilized to increase defense spending.

Harold Macmillan observed while Churchill attacked Labour's arms program: "he has used these days to give a demonstration of energy and vitality. He has voted in every division; made a series of brilliant little speeches; shown all his qualities of humor and sarcasm."[106] When Labour sought further to extend its control over steel production units in the February 1951 session of Parliament, Churchill questioned such action. Steel was crucial to arms manufacturing, and he asked, was it wise to seek such power "at a moment when harmony, smooth working and well-known contacts and organization are more than ever vital?"[107] The government was able to overcome his objections as its measures passed by a vote of 308 to 298. But two major newspapers praised Churchill's arguments. The liberal *Manchester Guardian* spoke of his "closely reasoned statement...done with Mr. Churchill's thoroughness." *The Times* praised him "for seeking to discover the motives behind" Labour's policy. "Is it necessary" asked *The Times* "to insure high production?"[108]

In March 1951, ill health removed one of the most important figures in Attlee's government as Ernest Bevin resigned from the Foreign Office, becoming briefly Lord Privy Seal. He died on April 14, 1951. British diplomatic historians have given him a high place in the pantheon of Foreign Secretaries, ranking him with Castlereagh, Canning, Palmerston and Salisbury. His successor was Herbert Morrison, but this shrewd manager of the Labour Party's M. P.'s was misplaced at the Foreign Office. He even referred to his new position in his *Autobiography* as "the most onerous peace-time job in government."[109] His American counterpart, Dean Acheson, found that Morrison "knew nothing of foreign affairs and had no feel for situations beyond the sound of Bow bells."[110] Morrison's appointment was indicative of the fact that the Labour Cabinet had grown elderly and weary. Its principal members had been in public life before 1941; they had been Churchill's wartime colleagues and had, by 1951, served in government office during the previous ten years of strain and crisis. One has to go back to the days of Pitt, Perceval, Liverpool and Castlereagh for such a precedent. Dalton even remarked to Attlee that the 1951 Cabinet looked like a "government of pensioners."[111]

Another blow to Labour's fortunes came when Bevan resigned from the government on April 21, 1951, after Chancellor Gaitskill's April bugdet had introduced charges for false teeth and eye glasses as part of the national health system.[112] Bevan, trying to bolster his standing among Labour leftwingers, publicly criticized the government for sacrificing free health care for arms.[113] The effect of Bevan's resignation and the loss of Bevin was stated by *The Times* of April 25, 1951: "Attlee knows no doubt that the life of his government cannot now be long; he must be conscious all the time of the other elder statesmen who are no longer by his side."[114]

Foreign policy issues have not been emphasized in this book up to this point, yet the importance of such developments warrants a brief description because of their impact on the next General Election. The role of oil in Britain's energy requirements grew more vital as coal supplies became more expensive in price and inadequate in quantity. The Anglo-Iranian Oil Company, a British-registered concern, had built the largest oil refinery in the world at Abadan, Iran (Persia), where a community of 4,500 British citizens had managed not only the production but also the marketing and distribution facilities of the company. In 1933, an agreement between the company and the government of Iran provided for increased company payments to Iran as the amount of oil and dividends paid by the company increased. But by 1949, the Iranians pressured the company for a fifty-fifty share of the profits, and by 1950 the Iranian Mayils began to advocate nationalization of the Anglo-Iran Oil firm. The situation began to escalate when on March 7, 1951, the Iran Prime Minister, General Razmara, who the British had grudgingly respected as a sincere nationalist, was assassinated by an extremist sect, the Fedayan-I-Islam. By April 27, 1951, the Government of Iran was led by Dr. Mohammed Mossadegh, an advocate of nationalizing the British Oil Company.

The Labour Government was put in an unenviable position of having to accept the principle of nationalization by the Iranians. It could hardly object if a foreign government "shared" its commitment to one of the central tenets of its political creed. In the Commons on May 1, 1951, Churchill asked the Foreign Minister for a statement on Iran and the supply of oil.[115] Herbert Morrison announced that: "We do not, of course, dispute the right of a Government to acquire property in their own country, but we cannot accept that the company's whole position in Persia should be radically altered by unilateral action."[116] Yet, on the next day, Mossadegh nationalized the Anglo-Iranian company. Clement Attlee then decided to submit the dispute to the International Court at the Hague, while company officials sent a mission of experts to Teheran in an attempt peacefully to settle the conflict. But by June 20, 1951, the Iranians had rejected the company's efforts, and Morrison then felt that what was needed was a "sharp and forceful action."[117]

Pressed by his colleagues, Churchill requested a debate on Iran but did not advocate "forceful action" as he would not be privy to the details of any military operation. Harold Macmillan noted that he "is also very conscious that Morrison and company are just waiting to fix the 'warmonger' accusation upon him."[118] By June 27, 1951, Churchill asked Attlee if a meeting would be possible when both the Prime Minister and the leader of the Opposition could discuss the Iranian crisis. Attlee agreed and, after this meeting, Churchill reviewed the conflict with the Tory M. P.'s in a meeting on June 28, 1951, with the 1922 Committee. The Tory leader: "spoke with great moderation and caution about Persia. It is clear he thinks there may be a change for the better and that it would be foolish for the Tory Party to 'stick its neck' out."[119] Events seemed to vindicate this cautious approach as Prime Minister Mossadegh next announced that he would meet in mid July with Averell Harriman, the American President's envoy, to discuss a possible end to the crisis.

When the Harriman mission failed, a full debate on the Middle East became inevitable. The gravity of the situation was again brought home to the British when on July 1, 1951, the Government of Egypt, still smarting because of its military defeat at the hands of the newly-formed Israeli state, ordered its warships to stop and board an English steamship, the *Empire Roach*, as the ship sailed through the Suez Canal on its way to the Israeli port of Aquaba.[120] The debate took place on July 30, 1951, but it was preceeded by a speech of the Foreign Secretary to a group of Durham miners on July 24, 1951. Herbert Morrison had spoken of "the

warlike fever of the Conservative backbenchers" and
"dangerous Tory irresponsibility in foreign affairs."[121]
Churchill's response to this speech showed his debating
strategy: to appear as the moderate who stood above party
politics. "Here is the new Foreign Secretary, who shows all
the world that his main thought in life is to be a caucus boss
and a bitter party electioneer."[122] The Conservatives, instead,
seek a bypartisan approach over the events in the Middle
East which "might help the Government and the general
policy of the country."[123] This was said to be the reason for
Churchill's meeting with Attlee on June 27th: "We have
endeavored to make the Government feel that a policy of
firmness, exercised with prudence, would in this matter...be
treated in a non-party spirit."[124] Addressing the Egyptian
seizure of the *Empire Roach*, Churchill stated that the Labour
Government should have used this incident to reappraise its
military aid policy to Cairo, especially in light of England's
contribution to that nation's defense during World War II:
"we preserved Egypt from the injury and pillage of Nazi-
Fascist subjugation."[125] Should the government continue to
send "ships of war, aeroplanes and other munitions, while
all they had to do, for their part, was to go on insulting us
ever more bitterly every day?"[126]

On Iran, Churchill described the crisis with Mossadegh as
one "calling, in an exceptional degree, for patience on the
basis of firmness."[127] Involved here was not a black/white
situation for although "the conduct of the Persian
Government has been outrageous, this must not lead us to
ignore what is fair and equitable in the Persian case."[128] He
then gave his support to future talks "which may
conceivably be protracted"[129] between London and Teheran
but which could reduce tensions and reach an equitable
agreement. However, "the Conservative Party will oppose
and censure by every means in their power the total
evacuation of Abadan."[130] The refinery must be staffed by a
sufficient "number of British Anglo-Persian personnel"[131] if
the operation of the installation is to be "re-started whenever

a settlement is reached."[132] What drew Labour cries of "warmonger" was Churchill's concluding remarks, "we must never agree to their [personnel] being withdrawn. If violence is offered to them, we must not hesitate to intervene, if necessary by force."[133]

The Labour M. P. for Coventry East, Richard Crossman, claimed that here was "the whole difference"[134] between Tory and Labour since the Tories "want the oil installations protected by military force. They say 'show the flag, use force, because that is the only language the lesser breeds understand.'"[135] The Tories countered by pressing Attlee for a statement on evacuation. The Prime Minister ended the debate with the words that there "may have to be a withdrawal from the oil wells and there may have to be a withdrawal from some part of Abadan, but our intention is not to evacuate entirely."[136] Both Churchill and Attlee had finished their remarks, but the term "warmonger" was to be a key election slogan.

The summer months of 1951 witnessed a further weakening of the economy. The oil crisis operated to increase Britain's need for dollar-oil imports. The record trade deficit of 150 million pounds for June 1951 was followed by a deficit of 127 million pounds in July. The gold and dollar deficit for July-September 1951 was $638 million, worse even than the same period of 1949.[137] By September 3, 1951, the butter and bacon ration was cut to three ounces, and cheese to one and a half ounces.[138] With his government harassed by problems in the Middle East and now facing yet another economic crisis, Attlee surprisingly announced the dissolution of Parliament on September 19th with polling day set for October 25th. As was true of the decision of January 1950, Morrison was not consulted by Attlee. When informed of the Prime Minister's announcement, Morrison did not display enthusiasm.[139] Events moved quickly. On October 2, 1951, all British managers and employees were expelled from Persian oil fields and from Abadan, this in spite of Attlee's statement to the Commons of July 30th.

Eight days later, anti-British riots broke in Egypt when the Cairo government denounced a treaty, signed in 1936, between England and Egypt, which had established Britain's rights in the Nile Valley and the system of "dual" control over the Sudan. Thus, the election of 1951 would be fought against a background of diplomatic and economic uncertainty.

Four months prior to the October General Election, the Conservative Research Department had worked on producing a draft of the party's next election manifesto. As the third full-length statement in three years, *Britain Strong and Free*, differed little from *This is the Road* or *Right Road for Britain*.[140] Between September 20-22, 1951, Churchill reviewed the draft with Butler, Woolton, Eden and Macmillan.[141] The finalized document mentioned familiar themes: the Iron and Steel Act repealed, nationalized industries were to be reviewed by a Monopolies Commission to insure fair pricing practices, and the Worker's Charter provisions of the *Industrial Charter* were to become part of British industrial relations. Churchill's introduction in the manifesto established the Tory theme of the 1951 election:

> Socialists have shown again and again their belief in an all-powerful central planning and organising authority governed by countless Rules and Regulations and ordering how the simplest of actions are to be carried out by the individual. Conservatives on the other hand hold that while the Government should guide, and establish general objectives and priorities, it should be the servant and not the master of the people.[142]

Britain Strong and Free used the slogan "Set the People Free," a phrase which emphasized Churchill's anti-control, less government rhetoric.[143] But this message did not advocate a "freedom from" the welfare state, as the Tory housing pledge of 300,000 homes a year was put forward as the party's major domestic program: "Our young people, wanting homes of their own, have watched their hopes fade as the waiting lists grow."[144] The high cost and scarcity of goods and services was also emphasized by the Conservatives. "Our housewives have gone on bravely trying to feed their families on two ounces of this or ten pennyworth of that. We have laughed off the slate in the coal bin, the gas that fails while the Sunday dinner is cooking, and the electricity that is cut at the most awkward moment.... Britain has deserved better than this."[145] Published on September 28, 1951, the Conservative manifesto intended to contest the election on domestic issues, but events were soon to alter this strategy.

The Annual Labour Party Conference began on October 1, 1951, at Scarborough. It soon became "apparent that it was the peace-or-war issue which most attracted the leaders and excited the delegates."[146] Labour entered the 1951 campaign with its left wing, led by Bevan, openly critical of the Government's rearmament program. This split was made even more apparent when at the conference, the party's controlling National Executive Committee held elections for its seven members, and four of the seven new members that were elected were Bevanites.[147] To avoid an electoral fissure among the ranks, Morrison, who again served as chief campaign strategist, astutely united his party by emphasizing Labour's foreign policy goal of "peace." This strategy was not unconnected with his role as Foreign Secretary.[148] The peace theme was translated at the conference into the following election slogan, first by Bevan: "I do not think that Winston Churchill wants war—but the trouble with him is that he does not know how to avoid it."[149] Joining Bevan, Morrison told the party faithful: "I do not accuse the average Conservative of being a warmonger, of thirsting for the shedding of blood, or of wishing to be involved needlessly in a world war.... But it is their temperament; it is the background of their mental outlook."[150] The party's manifesto also gave peace more attention than domestic issues. In his study of the 1951 general election, D. E. Butler found that in the 1950 campaign only 47 percent of the Labour M. P. candidate speeches contained any allusion to foreign affairs. In 1951, 93 percent made mention of this subject as Labour candidates "put it in the very forefront of their argument."[151] Likewise, nationalization, once Labour's major electoral theme, was not given prominence in its manifesto or campaign.

Only twenty nine members of the 1950 Parliament failed to seek election to its successor. In most constituencies candidates were opposed by the same individuals who stood in the 1950 contest. The major difference was the decline of the Liberal candidates, 475 in 1950 but only 109 office seekers in 1951, thus making the election in most constituencies a straightforward struggle between the Conservative and the Labour parties. London, the nation's largest urban center, was targeted by the Tories as they sought to capitalize on the housing issue among its urban voters. Also, the Liberal voters who had numbered some two and three fourths million in 1950, were wooed by the Conservatives who felt they had a good chance of increasing their vote in those constituencies which were not contested by the weakened Liberal Party.

In his first election speech of October 2, 1951, Churchill sought to diffuse the "peace or war" issue. Conscious of the evacuation of Abadan, his opening remarks were hard-hitting, "This decision convicts Mr. Attlee of breaking the solemn undertaking"[152] of July 30, 1951. Then he stated that his remark would soon by used by "Mr. Morrison, the Foreign Secretary, and all his party associates...to cover up their failure by saying that the Tories want war."[153] But this was a bogus issue—war over Abadan—because given the evacuation there "is no question of using force."[154] He next moved to the main thrust of his speech, domestic affairs: "What we need is a period of steady, stable administration by a broad-based Government...with the power to carry on a tolerant, non-partisan, non-doctrinaire system of policy."[155] Trying to appear above the party battle, Churchill concluded with the hope that the election: "will be no vindictive triumph for Tories over Socialists, no dull exclusion of

Liberal and independent forces, but rather a period of healing and revival."[156] Herbert Morrison responded on the next day and pursued the warmonger theme:

> Mr. Churchill said last night that the Prime Minister had broken his word...that he had said that we intended to stay in Southern Persia.
>
> ...But what he did not say was that he would use force in keeping our people in Abadan.... So you see that even in respect of Persia there is an implication of force in the mind of the Leader of the Opposition.[157]

However, Labour's strategy backfired when on October 8, 1951, the liberal *Manchester Guardian* published a series of documents showing that as late as September 22, 1951, the Government had turned down a Persian offer to reopen negotiations to settle the conflict.[158]

The *Manchester Guardian* article presented Churchill with a major question: should he aggresively challenge Labour on this foreign policy issue? His choice, stated in a national broadcast of October 8, 1951, was later described as the best Conservative broadcast of the election, perhaps Churchill's finest speech during the Opposition Years.[159] Instead of party strife, the Tory leader first asked for reconciliation: "we need not magnify our differences."[160] Keeping his course steady on the domestic front, Churchill next reviewed the Conservatives' historic commitment to social reform as he mentioned Butler's Education Act of 1944 and Lord Woolton's wartime White Papers on Employment. Labour's postwar commitment to nationalization had failed the nation because it had given inadequate services to consumers.[161] Instead of production and growth, the British economy was "hampered" and "fettered" by controls and restrictions. He then came to the pivotal part of his address:

> The differences between our outlook and the Socialist outlook on life is the difference between the ladder and queue. We are for the ladder. Let all try their best to climb. They are for the queue. Let each wait in his place till his turn comes. But, we ask, "What happens if anyone slips out of his place in the queue?" "Oh!" say

the Socialists," our officials—and we have plenty of them—come and put him back in it. And when they come back to us and say: "We have told you what happens if anyone slips out of the queue, but what is your answer to what happens if anyone slips off the ladder"? Our reply is: "We shall have a good net and the finest social ambulance service in the world."[162]

Absent from this speech were any throwbacks to the "Laski scares" or "Beaverbrook stunts" of the 1945 election. Winston Churchill projected a moderate, reasoned appeal, one that spoke of his party's concern and interest for domestic issues and of its support of the welfare state. Rab Butler wrote in his *Memoirs* that this address was Churchill's finest personal effort since the war.[163] The speech led to *The Times* endorsement of the Tories:

It is this new impetus, the freshness of mind and of spirit which a change of Government might be expected to bring...the choice between the Labour and Conservative parties today is a choice between a Cabinet utterly exhausted by six years in office, and an alternative Cabinet which has had the opportunity of refreshment afforded by six years spent in Opposition.[164]

Churchill's next three speeches were also centered on domestic issues. When the Labour leader, Arthur Deakin, publicly asked if a Conservative Government was contemplating new trade union legislation, Churchill reacted quickly to reassure the powerful union spokesman, on October 9, 1951 in Woodford: "The Conservative Party have no intention of initiating any legislation affecting trade unions, should we become responsible in the new Parliament. We hope to work with the trade unions in a loyal and friendly spirit."[165] The themes of less controls, inflated consumer prices and housing shortages formed the nucleus of his speech at St. Andrews Hall, Glasgow, on October 17, 1951. It began, "We do not accept the Socialist assertion and belief that the gentlemen in Whitehall know best."[166] A new Conservative Government would move quickly to implement its social reformist policies whose major domestic goal is "300,000 new houses a year."[167] He claimed that it had not been Conservative programs that have brought the "misery" and "overcrowding" to England's urban areas, but Labour's failure to achieve their 1945 election pledge of millions of new houses, "this shocking failure of the Socialists is surely one which now presents itself to the verdict and to the sentence of the nation."[168]

Clement Attlee followed Churchill to Glasgow. There, on October 22, 1951, just three days before polling day, he put his case to the voters. His message was that the rise in consumer prices could not be blamed on the Labour Government. This was the fault of economic forces beyond the control of his administration, such as the need for costly raw materials because of the demands of American and West European rearmament programs.[169] But the *Scotsman* of Glasgow wrote:

> The greatest weakness, however, in the Prime Minister's analysis of the domestic situation was his failure to show how appreciable improvements could be achieved. Thus he attributed the rise in prices mainly to world conditions and to factors outside the Government's control, which implies that he has no remedy.... The real remedy for our economic ills is increased productivity, but Mr. Attlee gave no indication of how this is to be achieved.[170]

Churchill's last speech at Home Park Football Ground, Plymouth, on October 23, 1951, dealt with the "warmonger" or "peace" issue:

> It is the opposite of the truth. If I remain in public life at this juncture it is because, rightly or wrongly, but sincerely, I believe that I may be able to make an important contribution to the prevention of a Third World War and to bringing nearer that lasting peace settlement which the masses of the people of every race and in every land...desire. I pray indeed that I may have this opportunity. It is the last prize I seek to win.[171]

In the campaign's last three days the Labour Party made one final attempt at selling its warmonger slogan when the *Daily Mail* ran a continuous headline of "Whose Finger on the Trigger?" A picture of a pistol was featured and its proximity to Churchill's photo was easily noted. He sued the paper for libel, and following the election was awarded a favorable out-of-court settlement. The proceeds were later given to a national charity.

The total voter turnout of 82.6 percent was only slightly below the record 83.9 percent of the 1950 election. The Conservatives secured 321 Parliamentary seats, Labour 295 and the Liberals six. The Tory victory was based on a minority of votes cast, a result that had occurred in 1929 and was to happen again in 1974. The Conservatives had 13,717,538 votes (48 percent); Labour received 13,948,605 (48.8 percent); and the Liberals 730,556 (2.5 percent). The Tories gained twenty-three new seats, twenty-one taken from Labour and two from the Liberals. Eleven of the twenty-one Conservative gains from Labour came from London and the southeast of England. But most of all, it was the ex-Liberal votes that assured the Tory victory. Of the twenty-one seats which the Conservatives took from Labour, 16 were seats where in 1950 the Liberal vote had exceeded the Labour majority and where in 1951 no Liberal candidate appeared.[172] By a six-to-four proportion, Liberals voted Tory in seats where there was no Liberal candidate in the 1951 election. Churchill's decision to play the "domestic card" paid a big dividend with these Liberal voters.[173]

Following the news of victory, Churchill did not express bitterness nor display resentment towards his Labourite opponents. Harold Macmillan records "Churchill bore no rancour. As usual, he passed from the conclusion of one event to face the next."[174] The politics of the Opposition Years had ended as Churchill and his Conservative Party, once again, grasped the levers of power.

Notes

[1]Frank K. Roberts, "Ernest Bevin as Foreign Secretary," in *The Foreign Policy of the British Labour Governments, 1945-1951*, Ritchie Ovendale, editor (Bath: Pitman Press, 1984), p. 23.

[2]H. G. Nicholas, *The British General Election of 1950* (London: Frank Cass and Company, Limited), p. 304.

[3]Conservative Research Department Files ("N") file, "A description of policy-making with WSC," March 1950, Notes for Lord Butler's *Memoirs* (Bodleian Library, Oxford University).

[4]Ibid.

[5]Macmillan, *Tides of Fortune*, p. 312.

[6]*The Times*, "The Labour Manifesto," January 18, 1950.

[7]James K. Pollock, ed., *British Election Studies, 1950* (Ann Arbor: The George Wahr Publishing Company, 1951), p. 3.

[8]Ibid., p. 19.

[9]Nicholas, *The British General Election of 1950*, p. 117.

[10]Butler Papers, RAB, H, 46, "The Conservative Research Department and Conservative Recovery After 1945," Memorandum, Michael Fraser to Mr. Butler, September 6, 1961 (Trinity College, Cambridge University), p. 5.

[11]"This is the Road," as published in *Conservatism, 1945-1950*, Conservative Political Centre (London: The Thanet Press, 1950), p. 227.

[12]Ibid., p. 230.

[13]Ibid., p. 231.

[14]Ibid., p. 235.

[15]"This is the Road," as published in *Conservatism, 1945-1950*, p. 231.

[16]Ibid., p. 232.

[17]Ibid.

[18]Nicholas, *The British General Election of 1950*, p. 4.

[19]Samuel J. Eldersfeld, "Patterns of Urban Dominance in British Election," in James K. Pollock, ed., *British Election Studies, 1950,*p. 82.

[20]Ibid., p. 81.

[21]Earl of Kilmuir, *Political Adventure*, p. 168.

[22]Nicholas, *The British General Election of 1950*, pp. 8-9.

[23]Pollock, *British Election Studies, 1950*, p. 3.

[24]Ibid., p. 65.

[25]Ibid.

[26]James, *Winston S. Churchill, His Complete Speeches, 1897-1963*, Vol. VIII, *1950-1963*, p. 7904.

[27]Ibid., p. 7905.

[28]Ibid.

[29]Ibid., p. 7906.

[30]Ibid.

[31]Ibid., p. 7908.

[32]Ibid.

[33]Ibid.

[34]Ibid., p. 7910.

[35]James, *Winston S. Churchill, His Complete Speeches, 1897-1963*, Vol. VIII, *1950-1963*, p. 7922.

[36]Ibid., p. 7926.

[37]Nicholas, *The British General Election of 1950*, p. 140.

[38]Ibid.

[39]Macmillan, *Tides of Fortune*, p. 313.

[40]James, *Winston S. Churchill, His Complete Speeches, 1897-1963*, Vol. VIII, *1950-1963*, p. 7931.

[41]Ibid., p. 7939.

[42]Ibid., p. 7948.

[43]*The Times*, "House of Commons, 1950," (London: Times Office, 1950), p. 20.

[44]Ibid.

[45]Ibid., see also, Bullock, *Ernest Bevin, Foreign Secretary, 1945-1951*, p. 756.

[46]*News Chronicle*, February 17, 1950.

[47]*News Chronicle*, "Election, Neck and Neck," February 22, 1950.

[48]Nicholas, *The British General Election of 1950*, p. 296.

[49]Morgan, *Labour in Power, 1945-1951*, p. 406.

[50]Samuel J. Eldersveld, "Patterns of Urban Dominance in British Elections," in James K. Pollock, ed.,*British Election Studies, 1950,*, p. 95.

[51]Ibid., p. 87.

[52]Ibid., p. 64.

[53]Michael Foot, *Aneurin Bevan, A Biography*, Vol. II, *1945-1960* (New York: Atheneum, 1974), p. 238.

[54]Herbert Morrison, *Autobiography* (Odham Press Limited, 1960), p. 264.

[55]Nicholas, *The British General Election of 1950*, p. 222.

[56]Blake, *The Conservative Party from Peel to Thatcher*, p. 263.

[57]James, *Winston S. Churchill, His Complete Speeches, 1897-1963*, Vol. VIII, *1950-1963*, p. 7910.

[58]Macmillan, *Tides of Fortune*, p. 316.

[59]Ibid., p. 318.

[60]Nigel Fisher, *Ian Macleod* (London: Andre Deutsch, 1973), p. 72.

[61]Ibid.

[62]Interview, Lord Fraser of Kilmorack, London, England, House of Lords, July 24, 2986.

[63]Earl of Kilmuir, *Political Adventure*, p. 171.

[64]Ibid., p. 167.

[65]Great Britain, Parliament, *Parliamentary Debates* (Commons), 5th Series, 472 (March 7, 1950): 141.

[66]Ibid., p. 619.

[67]Great Britain, Parliament, *Parliamentary Debates* (Commons), 5th Series, 474 (April 24, 1950): 621.

[68]Ibid., p. 619.

[69]Ibid.

[70]Woolton Papers, M. S. Woolton 21, Correspondence as Chairman, Conservative Party, Letter, Lord Woolton to Winston S. Churchill, May 2, 1950 (Bodleian Library, Oxford University).

[71]Ibid., May 10, 1950.

[72]Ibid.

[73]James, *Winston S. Churchill, His Complete Speeches, 1897-1963*, Vol. VIII, *1950-1963*, p. 8001.

[74]John Ramsden, *The Making of Conservative Party Policy, The Conservative Research Department since 1929* (London: Longman Group Limited, 1980), p. 151.

[75]Woolton Papers, M. S. Woolton 21, Correspondence as Chairman, Conservative Party, Letter, Robert Boothby to Lord Wolton, September 30, 1950 (Bodleian Library, Oxford University).

[76]Great Britain, Parliament, *Parliamentary Debates* (Commons), 5th Series, 478 (September 19, 1950): 1723.

[77]Ibid., p. 1792.

[78]Ibid., p. 1721.

[79]Attlee Papers, M. S. 133, 1950-1951 (Bodleian Library, Oxford University).

[80]Great Britain, Parliament, *Parliamentary Debates* (Commons), 5th Series, 478 (September 9, 1950): 1725-1726.

[81]Ibid., p. 1729.

[82]Great Britain, Parliament, *Parliamentary Debates* (Commons), 5th Series, 478 (March 7, 1950): 869.

[83]Conservative Research Department Files, Survey dated July 27, 1950, in "Policy Documents Papers, 1951," (Bodleian Library, Oxford University).

[84]Ibid.

[85]Lord Butler, *The Art of the Possible Memoirs*, p. 155.

[86]James, *Winston S. Churchill, His Complete Speeches, 1897-1963*, Vol. VIII, *1950-1963*, p. 8106.

[87]Conservative Research Department Files, "Business Committee, 1949-1956," (Bodleian Library, Oxford University).

[88]Great Britain, Parliament, *Parliamentary Debates* (Commons), 5th Series, 480 (November 6, 1950):699.

[89]Ibid., p. 700.

[90]Ibid., pp. 700-701.

[91]Ibid., p. 701.

[92]Ibid., p. 702.

[93]Ibid., p. 703.

[94]Ibid., p. 704.

[95]*Economic Survey for 1951*, Cmd 8195, April 1951, para. F.

[96]Blake, *The Decline of Power, 1915-1964*, p. 337.

[97]J. C. R. Dow, *The Management of the British Economy, 1945-1960* (Cambridge: University Press for NIESR, 1964), p. 64; see also Sir E. Boyle in J. K. Bowers, ed., *Inflation, Development and Integration* (Leeds: University Press, 1979), pp. 3-4.

[98]Michael Foot, *Aneurin Bevan*, Vol. II, *1945-1960* (London: David-Poynter, 1973), p. 299.

[99]*The Times*, "Coal Crisis," January 3, 1951.

[100]Attlee Papers, M. S. 133, 1950-1951 (Bodleian Library, Oxford University).

[101]Ibid.

[102]Attlee Papers, M. S. 133, 1950-1951 (Bodleian Library, Oxford University).

[103]Ibid.

[104]Great Britain, Parliament, *Parliamentary Debates* (Commons), 5th Series, 483 (January 29, 1951): 585.

[105]Ibid., p. 586.

[106]Macmillan, *Tides of Fortune*, p. 322.

[107]Great Britain, Parliament, *Parliamentary Debates* (Commons), 5th Series, 483 (February 7, 1951): 1752.

[108]*Manchester Guardian*, "The Government Wins Through," February 8, 1951; *The Times*, February 9, 1951.

[109]Morrison, *Autobiography*, p. 273.

[110]Acheson, *Present at the Creation*, p. 505.

[111]Morgan, *Labour in Power*, 1945-1951, p. 460.

[112]Great Britain, Parliament, *Parliamentary Debates* (Commons), 5th Series, 486 (April 10, 1950): 852.

[113]Attlee Papers, M. S. 133, 1950-1951 (Bodleian Library, Oxford University).

[114]*The Times*, "Cabinet Changes," April 25, 1956.

[115]Great Britain, Parliament, *Parliamentary Debates* (Commons), 5th Series, 487 (May 1, 1951): 1008.

[116]Ibid., p. 1012.

[117]Morrison, *Autobiography*, p. 282.

[118]Macmillan, *Tides of Fortune*, p. 345.

[119]Ibid., p. 346.

[120]Great Britain, Parliament, *Parliamentary Debates* (Commons), 5th Series, 490 (July 19, 1951): 1409.

[121]Great Britain, Parliament, *Parliamentary Debates* (Commons), 5th Series, 491 (July 30, 1951): 989.

[122]Ibid.

[123]Ibid., p. 992.

[124]Ibid.

[125]Ibid., p. 981.

[126]Ibid., p. 986.

[127]Ibid., p. 994.

[128]Ibid., p. 990.

[129]Ibid., p. 993.

[130]Ibid., p. 994.

[131]Ibid.

[132]Ibid.

[133]Ibid., p. 995.

[134]Ibid., p. 998.

[135]Ibid.

[136]Ibid., p. 1072.

[137]Morgan, *Labour in Power, 1945-1951*, p. 478.

[138]Ibid.

[139]B. Donoughue and G. W. Jones, *Herbert Morrison: Portrait of a Politician* (London: Weidenfeld and Nicolson, 1973), pp. 501-502.

[140]Butler Papers, RAB, H, 46, "The Conservative Research Department and Conservative Recovery After 1945," Memorandum, Michael Fraser to Mr. Butler, September 6, 1961 (Trinity College, Cambridge University), p. 8.

[141]Macmillan, *Tides of Fortune*, pp. 354-356.

[142]*Britain Strong and Free*, in *The New Conservatism, an Anthology of Post-War Thought* (London: Conservative Political Centre, 1955), pp. 57-58.

[143]Conservative Research Department Files, "Election Manifesto, 1951," (Bodleian Library, Oxford University).

[144]*Britain Strong and Free*, in *The New Conservatism, an Anthology of Post-War Thought*, p. 57.

[145]Ibid.

[146]H. G. Nicholas, "The British General Election of 1951," *American Political Science Review* 46 (1952): 400.

[147]D. E. Butler, *The British General Election of 1951* (London: Macmillan and Company, Ltd., 1952), p. 90.

[148]Nicholas, "The British General Election of 1951," p. 399.

[149]Butler, *The British General Election of 1951*, p. 121.

[150]Ibid.

[151]Ibid. p. 141.

[152]James, *Winston S. Churchill, His Complete Speeches, 1897-1963*, Vol. VIII, *1950-1963*, p. 8246.

[153]Ibid.

[154]Ibid.

[155]Ibid.

[156]Ibid.

[157]Butler, *The British General Election of 1951*, p. 113.

[158]Butler, *The British General Election of 1951*, p. 115.

[159]Ibid., p. 66; see also, Martin Gilbert, *Winston S. Churchill, 'Never Dispair', 1945-1965*, Vol. VIII (Boston: Houghton Mifflin Company, 1988), p. 644.

[160]James, *Winston S. Churchill, His Complete Speeches, 1897-1963*, Vol. VIII, *1950-1963*, p. 8254.

[161]Ibid., p. 8256.

[162]Ibid.

[163]Lord Butler, *The Art of the Possible*, pp. 66-67.

[164]*The Times*, "Polling Day," October 10, 1951.

[165]James, *Winston S. Churchill, His Complete Speeches, 1897-1963*, Vol. VIII, *1950-1963*, p. 8260.

[166]Ibid., p. 8275.

[167]Ibid., p. 8276.

[168]Ibid.

[169]Attlee Papers, M. S. 133, 1950-1951 (Bodleian Library, Oxford University).

[170]"Mr. Attlee's Campaign Speech," *The Scotsman*, October 22, 1951.

[171]James, *Winston S. Churchill, His Complete Speeches, 1897-1963*, Vol. VIII, *1950-1963*, p. 8282.

[172]Nicholas, "The British General Election of 1951," p. 404.

[173]Morgan, *Labour in Power, 1945-1951*, p. 486.

[174]Macmillan, *Tides of Fortune*, p. 362.

CHAPTER VIII

SUMMARY, FINDINGS, AND CONCLUSIONS

> The essence of leadership is the
> recognition of real need.
>
> James MacGregor Burns

On a warm July afternoon in 1986, the former Deputy Chairman of the Conservative Party, Lord Fraser of Kilmorack, was just about to conclude his interview with this writer. He paused and then told me that for many young Tories of the 1945-1951 era, Winston Churchill was a "great oak under which a younger generation grew up politically." Since then, I have repeatedly recalled this remark as I asked myself what Lord Fraser's phrase meant in terms of Churchill's relationship to the Conservative Party and how he led, or failed to lead, the Tories in the six year period following the Second World War.

It is said of oak trees that they possess unique root systems. Churchill's political "roots" were based on a distinct personality, one that allowed him to operate far beyond his own class and times. He was a habitual rebel or outsider, one not easily tied to a political party. The key lies in the fact that as a young man his mind had not been molded by the elitist university education that had shaped many moneyed young men of his day. A self-taught individual, Churchill's outlook would be critical of established philosophies or conventional dogmas. Also, in the domestic arena he would be greatly influenced by his own romanticized definition of the term

"Tory Democracy." This phrase appears periodically in speeches throughout his political career. Although scholars, such as Samuel Beer and Robert Blake, have given this term a more than adequate and objective definition, its importance for Churchill was that it allowed his questioning mind to accept the welfare state as it evolved in response to the social and economic changes of British industrial life. New or unconventional personalities and policies that addressed the problems of poverty, pensions or unemployment were not foreign to his nature, whether they were presented by an ambitious civil servant, like William Beveridge, or by a YMCA dissident, Harold Macmillan.

For most of his career, this political style repelled rather than attracted the great mass of the Conservative Party. In its hour of great need, when Neville Chamberlain's appeasement policy had been so ruthlessly cast aside by Hitler, the Tories did not readily turn to Churchill to serve as party leader. The war changed this relationship but left the Tories devoid of effective party structure and domestic policy. Churchill's disastrous election campaign in 1945 reflected what amounted to the then bankruptcy of Conservative political programs. Yet, it was out of this defeat that Churchill's style of questioning accepted truisms and procedures proved most effective. The Tories needed a fundamental "re-think" and a leader willing to begin the search for new approaches. Thus, his style, with its ability to disregard pat phrases and dated policies, was the catalyst for the Conservative renewal.

Unlike Robert Rhodes James, I conclude that Churchill was an effective Opposition leader. His effectiveness is best explained in terms of a unique *modus operandi* which was composed of three elements: selection, utilization and articulation. He alone chose Lord Woolton to rebuild the party's organizational structure. He wanted Woolton to sink the party's "roots" deep enough to tap local constituency enthusiasm. Lord Woolton had been a symbol of Churchill's wartime government's promise of state intervention to prevent postwar unemployment, and it would be this kind of personality that the party leader entrusted to reshape a contemporary Conservative image. Likewise, Churchill appointed Rab Butler to shift Conservative political thought away from its laissez-faire philosophy. The success of this choice is most noticeable when one compares the campaign literature of the 1945 General Election to that of 1950 or 1951. What emerged from this philosophical redirection was a definite commitment to address those problems of work and homes that reversed the results of the 1945 election defeat.

Winston Churchill not only selected talent, he utilized it. The Conservative Research Department developed during the 1945-1951 era into the "training ground" for the party's future M. P.'s and ministers. It was here that the young and the ambitious could think, question and argue. The intellectual sparks that were generated at this level were directly linked to the party leader's Parliamentary efforts, a connection that did much to foster a sense of participation in the attempt to regain government office. Talent rather than social position counted at the Conservative Research Department, a fact that augmented the effort by both Churchill and Woolton to build for the Tories a popular, democratic image. As the Conservative Research Department grew into a "shadow" civil service, it began to assure the party that the function of policy formulation would be systematic. Elections were to be contested by sophisticated manifestoes, not as in 1945, with *ad hoc* cliches. Political expression during this six year period following World War II was untouched by the demands of television imagery of our day. What a Clement Attlee or a Herbert Morrison said in Parliament, or how the Leader of the Opposition argued in the House of Commons served as the major vehicle of political communication and education. It was in this forum that Churchill applied the third element of his opposition strategy, the articulation of postwar Conservatism. What he sought to accomplish was the association of the demands of the welfare state with the policies and programs of the Conservative revival. Nationalization, the major creed of the Labour Government, was challenged not because it violated any free enterprise ideal, but because it failed in most sectors of the economy to provide for the efficient and humane management of postwar society. Housing, a recognized domestic need of the Opposition Years, was presented as the main concern of any future Tory government. Adroitly used to emphasize Labour's inability to solve a fundamental need, Churchill by 1951 had connected the housing problem with such basic issues as the shortage and price of social services and consumer goods. It was this linkage that ultimately deprived the Labour party of the seals of office.

It has been written that successful leadership is the recognition of needs and the formulation of solutions to satisfy such desires. Winston Churchill proved to be a "broad brush" leader as he allowed his associates to plan for and develop the crucial details of a distinctive political creed and organization when the need for this change was critical. Unlike his wartime premiership during which he dominated the implementation of strategy and tactics, in the 1945-1951 era a Woolton or a Butler was free to test the structural or philosophical redirection that they laboured so long and hard to achieve. Also, Churchill's leadership did not lack in mistakes or miscalculations. His 1945 "Gestapo" speech was a classic political blunder, just as his inability to achieve an important electoral victory in the 1949 South Hammersmith constituency failed his party. Still, his accomplishment was that new personalities were encouraged to develop novel programs and ideas which enriched postwar British Conservatism. The doubts that the English voter manifested in 1945 against the Tories as the party of privilege and laissez-faire economics and against Churchill as the spokesman of this kind of political philosophy began to fade. Returning to power in 1951, the Conservatives, under Churchill's last government, succeeded in building 350,000 homes a year by 1955, and in the General Election of that year, the party's Parliamentary majority rose to 67 over Labour. In conclusion, the new policies and organization the Conservatives adopted under Churchill's leadership during the Opposition Years enabled the party to emerge as a viable and dynamic political entity. Looked upon as a "beaten army" after the 1945 election, the Tories since 1951 have been in office thirty out of forty years and produced the unprecedented political "miracle" of a prime minister who achieved victory in three successive general elections.

BIBLIOGRAPHY

Papers and Collections

Attlee Papers. M. S. 131/132 (1937-1949) Bodleian Library, Oxford University, England

Brendan Bracken Papers. Churchill College, Cambridge University, England

Butler Papers. Trinity College, Cambridge University, England.

Lord Chandos Papers. Churchill College, Cambridge University, England.

Conservative Research Department Files. Bodleian Library, Oxford University, England.

Earl of Selborne Papers. Bodleian Library, Oxford University.

Woolton Papers. Bodleian Library, Oxford University, England.

Oral Histories and Reports

Blake, Lord Robert. The Queen's College, Oxford, July 17, 1986.

Colville, Sir John. Oral History, 32 Hyde Park Square, London, July 16, 1986.

Economic Survey for 1951, Cmd. 8195, April 1951, para. F.

Fraser, Lord of Kilmorack, C. B. E. Oral History, London, England, House of Lords, July 24, 1986.

James, Robert Rhodes. House of Commons, July 15, 1986.

Interim and Final Reports of the Committee on Party
Organization, 1948 and 1949, London, England.

Report of the 43rd Annual Conference of the Labour party,
December 11-15, 1944.

Social Insurance and Allied Services, Cmd. 6404.

68th Annual Conference Report of the Conservative Party,
1947.

Autobiographies , Memoirs and Speeches

Acheson, Dean. *Present at the Creation: My Years in the State
Department*. New York: W. W. Norton, Inc., 1969.

Amery, L. S. *My Political Life: the Unforgiving Years, 1929-
1940*. London: Hutchinson, 1953.

Butler, Lord. *The Art of the Possible: Memoirs*. Boston:
Gambit Inc., 1972.

Churchill, Winston S. *Great Destiny: Sixty Years of the
Century Recounted in His Own Incomparable Words*. New
York: G. P. Putnam's Sons, 1962.

Churchill, Winston S. *The Second World War*. Vol. II. *Their
Finest Hour*. Boston: Houghton Mifflin company, 1944.

Churchill, Winston S. *My Early Life: a Roving Commission*.
Glasgow: William Collins Sons and Company, Ltd.,
1930.

Churchill, Winston S. *The Unrelenting Struggle*. London:
Cassell, 1943.

Citrine, Lord. *Two Careers*. London: Hutchinson, 1967.

Croft, Sir Henry Page. *My Life of Strife*. London: Collins,
1948.

Colville, John. *The Fringes of Power, 10 Downing Street
Diaries, 1939-1955*. New York: W. W. Norton and
Company, 1985.

Cross, J. A. *Lord Swinton*. Oxford: Clarendon Press, 1982.

Dalton, Lord (Hugh Dalton). *High Tide and After*. London:
Frederick Muller, 1962.

Dilks, David, ed. *The Diaries of Sir Alexander Cadogan OM,
1938-1945*. London: Putnam, 1971.

Eden, Anthony; Earl of Avon. *Memoirs, the Reckoning*. Vol. 4. Boston: Houghton Mifflin Company, 1955.

Harvie-Watt, G. S. *Most of My Life*. London: Collins, 1980.

Haxey, Simon. *Tory M. P*. London: Bictor Gollanez, Ltd., 1939.

James, Robert Rhodes, ed. *Chips: the Diaries of Sir Henry Channon*. London: Weidenfeld and Nicolson, 1967.

James, Robert Rhodes. *Winston S. Churchill, His Complete Speeches, 1897-1963*. Vol. I. *1857-1908*. New York: Chelsea House Publishers, 1974.

James, Robert Rhodes. *Winston S. Churchill, His Complete Speeches, 1897-1963*. Vol. II. *1908-1913*. New York: Chelsea House Publishers, 1974.

James, Robert Rhodes. *Winston S. Churchill, His Complete Speeches, 1897-1963*. Vol. VII. *1943-1949*. New York: Chelsea House Publishers, 1974.

James, Robert Rhodes, ed. *Winston S. Churchill, His Complete Speeches, 1897-1963*. Vol. VIII, *1950-1963*. New York: Chelsea House Publishers, 1974.

Jay, D. P. T. *Change and Fortune*. London: Hutchinson, 1980.

Jones, Thomas. *A Diary with Letters, 1931-1950*. London: Oxford University Press, 1954.

Kennan, George F. *Memoirs, 1925-1950*. Boston: Little, Brown and Company, 1967.

Kilmuir, Earl of. *Political Adventure, the Memoirs of the Earl of Kilmuir*. London: Weidenfeld and Nicolon, 1964.

Macmillan, Harold. *The Past Masters: Politics and Politicians, 1906-1939*. New York: Harper and Row, 1975.

Macmillan, Harold. *Tides of Fortune, 1945-1955*. London: Macmillan, 1969.

Morrison, Herbert. *Autobiography*. London: Odhams, 1960.

Nicolson, Nigel, ed. *Harold Nicolson: Diaries and Letters, The War Years, 1939-1945*. New York: Atheneum, 1967.

Priestley, J. B. *Postcripts*. London: Heineman, 1940.

Salter, Lord. *Memoirs of a Public Servant*. London: Faber and Faber, 1961.

Shinwell, Lord. *Conflict Without Malice*. London: Odhams Press, 1955.

Templewood, Viscount. *Nine Troubled Years*. London: Collins, 1954.

Wheeler-Bennett, Sir John, ed. *Action This Day. Working with Churchill: Memoirs by Lord Normanbrook, John Colville, Sir John Martin, Sir Ian Jacob, Lord Bridges, Sir Leslie Rowan*. London: Macmillan, 1968.

Williams, Philip M., ed. *The Diary of Hugh Gaitskill 1945-1956*. London: Jonathan Cope, 1983.

Winterton, Earl. *Orders of the Day*. London: Cassell and Company, Ltd., 1953.

Woolton, Earl of. *Memoirs*. London: Cassell, 1959.

Biographies

Blake, Robert. *Disraeli*. New York: Anchor Books, 1968.

Blake, Robert, *The Unknown Prime Minister: The Life and Times of Andrew Bonar Law, 1858-1923*. London: St. Martin's Press, 1955.

Brood, Lewis. *Winston Churchill*. Vol. I. *The Years of Preparation, a Biography*. New York: Hawthorne Books, 1958.

Bullock, Alan. *Ernest Bevin, Foreign Secretary, 1945-1951*. New York: W. W. Norton and Company, 1983.

Churchill, Randolph S. *Winston S. Churchill*. Vol. I. *Youth., 1874-1900*. Boston: Houghton Mifflin Company, 1966.

Churchill, Randolph S. *Winston S. Churchill*. Vol. II. *Young Statesman. 1901-1914*. Boston: Houghton Miffling Company, 1967.

Churchill, Winston S. *Lord Randolph Churchill*. Vol. I. London: Macmillan Company, 1906.

Colville, John. *Winston Churchill and His Inner Circle*. New York: Wyndham Books, 1981.

Donoughue, B., and Jones, G. W. *Herbert Morrison: Portrait of a Politician*. London: Weidenfeld and Nicolson, 1973.

Feiling, Keith. *The Life of Neville Chamberlain*. London: Macmillan and Company Ltd., 1946.

Fisher, Nigel. *Harold Macmillan*. New York: St. Martin's Press, 1982.

Fisher, Nigel. *Ian Macleod*. London: Arndre Deutsch, 1973.

Foot, Michael. *Aneurin Bevan*. Vol. II. *1945-1960*. London: Davis-Poynter, 1973.

Gilbert, Martin. *Winston S. Churchill*. Vol. VI. *Finest Hour, 1939-1941*. Boston: Houghton Mifflin Company, 1983.

Gilbert, Martin. *Winston S. Churchill*. Vol. V. *the Prophet of Truth, 1922-1939*. Boston: Houghton Mifflin Company, 1977.

Gilbert, Martin. *Winston S. Churchill*. Vol. VII. *Road to Victory, 1941-1945*. Boston: Houghton Mifflin Company, 1986.

Gilbert, Martin. *Winston S. Churchill*. 'Vol. VIII. *"Never Despair," 1945-1965*. Boston: Houghton Mifflin Company, 1988.

Harris, Kenneth. *Attlee*. London: Weidenfeld and Nicolson, 1982.

Horne, Alistair. *Harold Macmillan*. Vol. I. *1894-1956*. New York: Viking Pinguin Inc., 1989.

Humes, James C. *Churchill: Speaker of the Century*. New York: Stein and Day, 1982.

Hutchinson, George. *Edward Heath: A Personal and Political Biography*. London: Longman, 1970.

James, Robert Rhodes, M. P. "Churchill, the Man." *The Fifth Crosby Kemper Lecture, April 27, 1986*. Winston Churchill Memorial, Westminster College, Fulton, Missouri.

James, Robert Rhodes. *Churchill: a Study in Failure 1900-1939*. London: Weidenfeld and Nicolson, 1970.

James, Robert Rhodes. *Lord Randolph Churchill*. London: Weidenfeld and Nicolson, 1959.

Lysaght, Charles Edward. *Brendan Bracken*. London: Allen Lane, 1979.

Middlemans, Keith and Barnes, John. *Baldwin*. London: Weidenfeld and Nicolson, 1969.

Monypenny, W. F., and Buckle, G. E. *The Life of Benjamin Disraeli, Earl of Beaconsfield*. 2nd rev. ed. London: 1929

Morgan, Ted. *Churchill: Young Man in a Hurry, 1874-1915.* New York: Simon and Schuster, 1982.

Roberts, Carl. *Lord Birkenhead, Being an Account of the life of F. S. Smith, First Earl of Birkenhead.* New York: George H. Doran Company, 1938.

Rowse, A. L. *The Churchills: From the Death of Marlborough to the Present.* New York: Harper and Brothers, 1958.

Soames, Mary. *Clementine Churchill.* Boston: Houghton Mifflin, 1979.

Taylor, A. J. P. *Beaverbrook.* London: Hanush Hamilton, 1972.

Wheeler-Bennett, John H. *King George VI: His Life and Reign.* New York: St. Martin's Press, 1965.

Young, G. M. *Stanley Baldwin.* London: Rupert Hart-Davis, 1952.

Young, Kenneth. *Churchill and Beaverbrook, A Study in Friendship and Politics.* New York: James H. Heineman, Inc., 1966.

Monographs

Aldcroft, Derek H. *The Inter-War Economy.* London: Batsford, 1970.

Beveridge, Janet. *Beveridge and His Plan.* London: Hadder and Stoughton, 1954.

Barker, Anthony and Rush, Michael. *The Member of Parliament and His Information.* London: Allen and Unwin, 1970.

Beer, Samuel H. *Modern British Politic: A Study of Parties and Pressure Groups.* 2nd ed. London: Faber and Faber, 1969.

Butler, D. E. *The British General Election of 1951.* London: Macmillan and Company, Ltd., 1952.

Cairncross, Alec. *Years of Recovery:British Economic Policy, 1945-1951.* London: Methuen, 1985.

Chester, Sir Norman. *The Nationalisation of British Industry, 1945-1951.* London: His Majesty's Stationary Office, 1975.

Dow, J. C. R. *The Management of the British Economy 1945-1960*. Cambridge: University Press for NIESR, 1964.

Gardner, Richard N. *Sterling-Dollar Diplomacy*. Oxford: University Press, 1956.

Gilbert, Bentley, B. *British Social Policy 1918-1939*. London: Batsford, 1970.

Goodhart, Philip with Ursula Branston. *The 1922: the Story of the Conservative Backbenchers' Parliamentary Committee*. London: Macmillan, 1973.

Hoffman, J. D. *The Conservative Party in Opposition 1945-1951*. London: Macgibbon and Kee, 1964.

Keynes, John Maynard. *The General Theory of Employment, Interest and Money*. London: Macmillan, 1936.

McCallum, R. B., and Readman, Alison. *The British General Election of 1945*. London: Oxford University Press, 1947.

Pollard, Sidney. *The Development of the Modern British Economy, 1914-1950*. London: Edward Arnold, 1968.

Morgan, Kenneth O. *Labour in Power, 1945-1951*. Oxford: Clarendon Press, 1984.

Nicholas, H. G. *The British General Election of 1950*. London: Frank Cass and Company, 1968.

Taylor, A. J. P., ed. *Churchill Revised: a Critical Assessment*. New York: The Dial Press, Inc., 1969.

Taylor, A. J. P. ed., *Lord Beaverbrook, the Abdication of King Edward VIII*. New York: Atheneum, 1966.

General Books

Auden, W. H. *Poems*, 1930.

Barker, Elisabeth. *The British Between the Superpowers, 1945-1950*. Toronto: University of Toronto Press, 1983.

Blake, Robert. *The Conservative Party from Peel to Thatcher*. London: Fontana Press, 1985.

Blake, Robert. *The Decline of Power, 1915-1964*. London: Paladine Books, 1986.

Boothby, Robert; de v. Loder, John; Macmillan, Harold; and Stanley, Oliver. *Industry and the State: A Conservative View*. London: Macmillan, 1927.

Butler, David and Freeman, Jennie. *British Political Facts, 1900-1967*. London: Macmillan, 1968.

Butler, Lord, ed. *The Conservatives: A History from Their Origins to 1965*. London: George Allen and Unwin, Ltd., 1977.

Cecil, Lord Hugh. *Conservatism*. London: Home University Library, 1912.

Churchill, Winston S. *Liberalism and the Social Problem*. London: Hodder and Stoughton, 1909.

Ensor, R. C. K. *England 1870-1914*. Oxford: Clarendon Press, 1935.

Gardiner, A. G. *Pillars of Society*. London: J. M. Dent and Sons, Ltd., 1926.

Germains, Victor Wallace. *The Tragedy of Winston Churchill*. London: Hutchinson Company, 1932.

Gilbert, Felix. *The End of the European Era, 1890 to the Present*. 3rd ed. New York: W. W. Norton.

Hodson, J. L. *The Sea and the Land*. London: Gollanez, 1945.

Laski, Harold. *Where Do We Go From Here?* Harmondsworth: Penguin, 1940.

Lindsay, T. F., and Harrington, Michael. *The Conservative Party*. London: Macmillan, 1974.

Marwick, Arthur. *Britain in the Century of Total War, War and Peace and Social Change, 1900-1967*. Boston: Little, Brown, 1968.

McKenzie, Robert Trelford. *British Political Parties: The Distribution of Power within the Conservative and Labour Parties*. 2nd ed. New York: Praeger, 1964.

Mowat, C. L. *Britain Between the Wars 1918-1949*. Chicago: University of Chicago Press, 1955.

Pelling, Henry. *Modern Britain, 1885-1955*. New York: W. W. Norton Company, 1966.

Ramsden, John. *The Making of Conservative Party Policy, The Conservative Research Department Since 1929*. London: Longman Group Limited, 1980.

Ross, J. F. S. *Parliamentary Representation*. London: Eyre and Spottiswoode, 1943.

Rothwell, Victor. *Britain and the Cold War, 1941-1947*.
London: Jonathan Cope, 1982.

Runciman, W. G. *Relative Deprivation and Social Justice*.
London: Roultedge and Paul Kegan, 1966.

Skidelsky, Robert. *Politicians and the Slump*. London:
Macmillan, 1967.

Taylor, A. J. P. *English History, 1914-1945*. New York:
Oxford University Press, 1965.

Youngson, A. J. *The British Economy, 1920-1957*.
Cambridge: Harvard University Press, 1960.

Articles and Essays

Berrington, Hugh. "Conservative Party." *Political Quarterly*
32 (1961):373.

"Boyle, Sir E." In *Inflation, Development and Integratio*.
Edited by J. K. Bowers. Leeds: University Press, 1979,
pp. 3-4.

Bulmer-Thomas, Ivor. "How Conservative Policy is
Formed." *Political Quarterly* 24:2 (1953).

Butler, D. E. "Conservative Policy." *Political Quarterly* 20
(1949).

Butler, R. A. "A Disraelian Approach to Modern Politics."
In *Tradition and Change: Nine Oxford Lectures*. Edited by
R. A. Butler, et al. London: Conservative Political
Centre, 1954.

Cantwell, Frank V. "The Meaning of the British Election."
Public Opinion Quarterly 9 (1945).

Clarke, David. "The Organization of Political Parties."
Political Quarterly 21 (1950).

Eldersveld, Samuel J. "Patterns of Urban Dominance in
British Elections." In *British Election Studies, 1950*. Edited
by James K. Pollock. Ann Arbor: George Wahr
Publishing Company, 1951.

Epstein, Leon D. "Politics of British Conservatism."
American Political Science Review 48 (1954).

Harrison, Tom. "Should Leaders Lead?" *New Statesman*
(July 13, 1940).

Harrison, Tom. "Who'll Win?" *Political Quarterly* 15 (1948).

Keynes, J. M. "The Return Towards Gold." *The Nation* (February 21, 1925).

Milne, R. S. "Britain's Economic Planning Machinery." *American Political Science Review* 46 (1952):406.

Nicholas, H. G. "The British General Election of 1951." *American Political Science Review* 46 (1952).

Radzenowica, Sir Leon. "Some Preliminary Reflections of the Evaluation of Criminal Justice." *Virginia Law Review* 63 (1977).

Rose, Richard. "The Variability of Party Government."*Political Studies* 18 (1969):429.

Rubin, Merle. "Review of Martin Gilbert's *Winston S. Churchill*. Vol. VII. *Road to Victory, 1941-1945*." *Christian Science Monitor*, January 20, 1987.

Williams, D. "London and the 1931 Financial Crisis." *Economic History Review* 15:2 (1963).

Conservative Party Publications

"Britain Strong and Free." In *The New Conservatism, an Anthology of Post-War Thought*. London: Conservative Political Centre, 1955.

Butler, R. A. *Our Way Ahead*. London: Conservative Political Centre, 1956.

Butler, R. A. *Fundamental Issues* (A Statement on the Future Work of the Conservative Education Movement). London: Conservative Political Centre, 1946.

Conservatism, 1945-1950. London: Conservative Political Centre, 1950.

Forty Years of Progress. Post-War Problems. London: Central Committee, June 1945.

Macmillan, Harold. *The Middle Way: 20 Years After*. London: Conservative Political Centre, 1946.

The New Conservatism. London: Conservative Political Centre, 1955.

Debates

Great Britain, Parliament, Parliamentary Debates (Commons), 5th Series, 386.

Great Britain, Parliament, Parliamentary Debates (Commons), 5th Series, 404.

Great Britain, Parliament, Parliamentary Debates (Commons), 5th Series, 413.

Great Britain, Parliament, Parliamentary Debates (Commons), 5th Series, 414.

Great Britain, Parliament, Parliamentary Debates (Commons), 5th Series, 416.

Great Britain, Parliament, Parliamentary Debates (Commons), 5th Series, 417.

Great Britain, Parliament, Parliamentary Debates (Commons), 5th Series, 433.

Great Britain, Parliament, Parliamentary Debates (Commons), 5th Series, 439.

Great Britain, Parliament, Parliamentary Debates (Commons), 5th Series, 441.

Great Britain, Parliament, Parliamentary Debates (Commons), 5th Series, 443.

Great Britain, Parliament, Parliamentary Debates (Commons), 5th Series, 445.

Great Britain, Parliament, Parliamentary Debates (Commons), 5th Series, 457.

Great Britain, Parliament, Parliamentary Debates (Commons), 5th Series, 458.

Great Britain, Parliament, Parliamentary Debates (Commons), 5th Series, 460.

Great Britain, Parliament, Parliamentary Debates (Commons), 5th Series, 466.

Great Britain, Parliament, Parliamentary Debates (Commons), 5th Series, 468.

Great Britain, Parliament, Parliamentary Debates (Commons), 5th Series, 472.

Great Britain, Parliament, Parliamentary Debates (Commons), 5th Series, 474.

Great Britain, Parliament, Parliamentary Debates (Commons), 5th Series, 478.

Great Britain, Parliament, Parliamentary Debates (Commons), 5th Series, 480.

Great Britain, Parliament, Parliamentary Debates (Commons), 5th Series, 483.

Great Britain, Parliament, Parliamentary Debates (Commons), 5th Series, 486.

Great Britain, Parliament, Parliamentary Debates (Commons), 5th Series, 487.

Great Britain, Parliament, Parliamentary Debates (Commons), 5th Series, 490.

Great Britain, Parliament, Parliamentary Debates (Commons), 5th Series, 491.

Great Britain, Parliament, Parliamentary Debates (Lords), 4th Series, 32.

Great Britain, Parliament, Parliamentary Debates (Lords), 4th Series, 34.

Newspapers

Birmingham Post, June 26, 1945.
Daily Express," Under Which Flag," May 12, 1947.
Daily Express, June 20, 1945.
Daily Herald, 17, 1943.
Economist, October 12, 1946.
Economist, "The Tory Alternative," July 30, 1949.
The Elector, October 1937, p. 4.
Evening Standard, "Change of Heart," May 12, 1947.
Glasgow Herald, June 29, 1945.
The Listener, June 7, 1945, p. 629.
The Listener, June 14, 1945, p. 616.
The Listener, June 21, 1945, p. 688.
[London]*Times*, April 10, 1945.
Times, June 15, 1945.
Times, June 16, 1945.
Times, June 18, 1945.
Times, June 20, 1945.

Times, June 25, 1945.

Times, "Can the Conservative Win?" June 20, 1948.

Times, "The Labour Manifesto," January 18, 1950.

Times, "Coal Crisis," January 3, 1951.

Times, "The Government Wins Through," February 9, 1951.

Times, "Polling Day," October 10, 1951.

Times [Butt, Ronald], "Tory Civil Service," 20 December 1969.

Manchester Guardian, "The New Toryism," May 12, 1947.

Manchester Guardian, July 25, 1947.

Manchester Guardian, "Shanklin," February 26, 1949.

Manchester Guardian, "Tory Socialism?" July 23, 1949.

Manchester Guardian, February 8, 1951.

News Chronicle, June 11, 1945.

News Chronicle, August 14, 1945.

News Chronicle, February 17, 1959.

News Chronicle, "Election, Neck and Neck," February 22, 1950.

The Scotsman, "Mr. Attlee's Campaign Speech," October 22, 1951.

Spectator, November 12, 1943.

Spectator, "Tory Programme," May 16, 1947.

Spectator, "Right Road?" July 24, 1949.

Yorkshire Post, "A Better Plan for Every Man," May 12, 1947.

APPENDIX

QUESTIONNAIRE

1. Did the Conservative Party experience a fundamental change or renewal during the period 1945-1951?

2. What were the major stages or phases of the renewal?

3. Were the most important changes brought about by Churchill?

4. Can it be said that the changes in the Tory Party occurred at two levels: structural—in terms of party organization and membership—and philosophical/policy wise?

5. Were the structural changes the work of Lord Woolton? or Churchill? and/or others?

6. Were the philosophical/policy changes led by Butler? or by Churchill? and/or others?

7. Did Churchill philosophically accept his party's renewal efforts? Did he give the lead or were such changes forced on him by either Lord Woolton or Butler or both? Were such changes accepted by Churchill because of political expediency?

INDEX